P9-BZF-557

SET MY
HEART
ON FIRE

SET MY
HEART
ON FIRE

CATHERINE MARTIN

HARVEST HOUSE PUBLISHERS

EUGENE, OREGON

Unless otherwise indicated, all Scripture quotations are taken from the New American Standard Bible®, © 1960, 1962, 1963, 1968, 1971, 1972, 1973, 1975, 1977, 1995 by The Lockman Foundation. Used by permission. (www.Lockman.org)

Verses marked NLT are taken from the *Holy Bible,* New Living Translation, copyright © 1996. Used by permission of Tyndale House Publishers, Inc., Wheaton, IL 60189 USA. All rights reserved.

Verses marked NIV are taken from the HOLY BIBLE, NEW INTERNATIONAL VERSION®. NIV®. Copyright © 1973, 1978, 1984 by the International Bible Society. Used by permission of Zondervan. All rights reserved.

Verses marked AMP are taken from The Amplified Bible, Copyright © 1954, 1958, 1962, 1964, 1965, 1987 by The Lockman Foundation. All rights reserved. Used by permission. (www.Lockman.org)

Verses marked PHILLIPS are taken from J.B. Phillips: The New Testament in Modern English, Revised Edition. © J.B. Phillips 1958, 1960, 1972. Used by permission of Macmillan Publishing Company.

Scripture quotations marked "Phillips" are taken from The New Testament in Modern English, copyright © 1958, 1959, 1960 J.B. Phillips and 1947, 1952, 1955, 1957 The Macmillian Company, New York. Used by permission. All rights reserved.

Verses marked TLB are taken from *The Living Bible,* Copyright © 1971. Used by permission of Tyndale House Publishers, Inc., Wheaton, IL 60189 USA. All rights reserved.

Verses marked NCV are taken from *The Holy Bible, New Century Version,* Copyright © 1987, 1988, 1991 by Word Publishing, Nashville, TN 37214. Used by permission.

Verses marked CEV are taken from the Contemporary English Version © 1991, 1992, 1995 by American Bible Society. Used with permission.

Verses marked MSG are taken from The Message. Copyright © by Eugene H. Peterson 1993, 1994, 1995, 1996, 2000, 2001, 2002. Used by permission of NavPress Publishing Group.

Verses marked "Williams" are taken from the *Williams New Testament in the Language of the People.* Copyright © 1995, Charlotte Williams Sprawls, all rights reserved.

Every effort has been made to locate the owners of copyrighted materials in this publication. Upon notification, the publisher will make proper correction in subsequent printings.

Catherine Martin: Published in association with the literary agency of WordServe Literary Group, Ltd., 10152 S. Knoll Circle, Highlands Ranch, CO 80130

Cover by Koechel Peterson & Associates, Inc., Minneapolis, Minnesota

Cover photo © Adrian Moisei / iStockphoto

SET MY HEART ON FIRE

Copyright © 2008 by Catherine Martin
Published by Harvest House Publishers
Eugene, Oregon 97402
www.harvesthousepublishers.com

Library of Congress Cataloging-in-Publication Data
    Martin, Catherine, 1956-
    Set my heart on fire / Catherine Martin.
       p. cm.
    ISBN-13: 978-0-7369-2056-8
    ISBN-10: 0-7369-2056-0
    1. Holy Spirit—Textbooks. 2. Devotional literature. I. Title.
    BT121.3.M28 2007
    248.4—dc22

2007020552

All rights reserved. No part of this publication may be reproduced, stored in a retrieval system, or transmitted in any form or by any means—electronic, mechanical, digital, photocopy, recording, or any other—except for brief quotations in printed reviews, without the prior permission of the publisher.

Printed in the United States of America

07 08 09 10 11 12 13 14 15 16 / VP-SK / 13 12 11 10 9 8 7 6 5 4 3 2 1

Dedicated to my beloved husband,
David Martin,
who has taught me to be faithful
and responsible to what God has given me to do.
Thank you, David, for these first 25 years.
May God give us another 25, and may we,
by the grace of God, together experience more and more
the mighty power of the Holy Spirit in our lives.

*You will receive power when the Holy Spirit
has come upon you; and you shall be
My witnesses both in Jerusalem, and in all Judea and
Samaria, and even to the remotest part of the earth.*

ACTS 1:8

*[May He] grant you, according to the riches of
His glory, to be strengthened with power through
His Spirit in the inner man, so that Christ may
dwell in your hearts through faith.*

EPHESIANS 3:16-17

*Were not our hearts burning within us while
He was speaking to us on the road,
while He was explaining the Scriptures to us?*

LUKE 24:32

CONTENTS

Week One: God Has a Plan for You

Week Two: The Person of the Holy Spirit

Week Three: The Presence of the Holy Spirit

Week Four: The Power of the Holy Spirit

Week Five: The Purpose of the Holy Spirit

FOREWORD

My friend Catherine Martin is a walking, talking, teaching compendium of biblical knowledge. In this book she shares potent, practical, and powerful teaching on the Holy Spirit. The subtitle of this book could easily be "everything you wanted to know about the Holy Spirit but never got around to asking."

Catherine artfully weaves biblical teaching on the Holy Spirit around the teaching of great Bible scholars long forgotten in today's world. Her ability to challenge and convince us that the Holy Spirit ignites the power available to every believer will keep you turning the pages.

Hudson Taylor, a great missionary and statesman of another era, said, "The power given is not a gift from the Holy Spirit. He Himself is the power. Today He is as truly available and as mighty in power as He was on the day of Pentecost." In a warm and convincing manner, this book will bear out that truth in a way that can impact the life of every one of us.

Get ready to have your life changed as you read, think, and act upon the challenges Catherine presents in this book. Her gift of teaching makes us want to stretch and grow as we are empowered by the Holy Spirit.

Jim Smoke
author, speaker, life coach

His Lamp Am I

His lamp am I
To shine where He shall say.
And lamps are not for sunny rooms,
Nor for the light of day;
But for dark places of the earth,
Where shame and wrong and crime have birth;
Or for the murky twilight gray,
Where wandering sheep have gone astray;
Or where the light of faith grows dim
And souls are groping after Him;
And sometimes a flame,
Clear shining through the night,
So bright we do not see the lamp,
But only see the light.
So may I shine—His light the flame—
That men may glorify His name.

Annie Johnson Flint

INTRODUCTION

Thirty years ago I made a decision that changed my life. I was attending Arizona State University and living in an apartment with three girls who were friends from high school. One of my roommates was committed to Jesus Christ and lived for Him. I was living for myself and was not impressed by religion.

One day, Peggy, the former captain of our high school cheerleading squad, visited us in our apartment. Peggy was unlike most people I knew; she had a vibrant spirit and a love and kindness that reached all the way to my heart. Peggy was what I called an "on fire for the Lord" Christian. To me, Peggy seemed perfect. I thought, *I could never be like her. She has a peace I don't understand. She knows where she's going. And she knows what life is all about.*

Peggy's visit left a powerful impression on me. I couldn't quit thinking about her. Her walk with Christ would come into my mind at the most inopportune times—at a party, in class, or when I was out on a date. Eventually, I began thinking about the truth she embraced, and more importantly, the person she represented—the Lord Jesus Christ. The words of Jesus in John 14:6 that she had shared with me kept surfacing in my thoughts: "I am the way, and the truth, and the life; no one comes to the Father but through Me." I realized that if He is the truth,

I must live for Him. Living for anything but the truth seemed to me an incredibly irrational choice; why live for a lie! That is when I made the most important decision of my life—I surrendered my whole body, mind, and soul to the Lord Jesus Christ. My life has not been the same since that decision; it changed from merely a meaningless journey to an exciting adventure—the great adventure of knowing God.

I began attending church with a friend. I even bought a Bible and actually began reading it. And all that summer, I could not get something out of my mind—a Campus Crusade for Christ resource table I had seen on campus. I now know that was the leading of the Holy Spirit. I resolved to go to that table on the first day of the new school year and find out about Campus Crusade for Christ. That was the day I met Leann, a staff member with Campus Crusade, sitting all alone behind a simple table. I walked right up to her with a challenge: "What's this Campus Crusade all about?"

She stared at me for a few moments, giving me the once-over before a smile broadened on her face. Then she said calmly, "You'll need to make an appointment with me to discuss the opportunities."

I remember standing there, hearing her words, exasperation building up inside of me. "I want to do it all now," I heard myself say to her.

She looked surprised but pleased and eventually told me about three levels of commitment: College Life, Leadership Training Class, and Action Groups. "Which of these would you like to do?"

I knew the Holy Spirit was leading me when I responded, "I want to do it all!" Well, Leann's wisdom guided my young exuberance, and am I glad it did.

I started with the beginning Leadership Training Class taught by Elmer Lappen, one of the original staff members of Campus Crusade and director of the ministry at Arizona State University. At first, I wondered how he could effectively teach a class as he was confined to a wheelchair with crippling arthritis. I could see he was in terrible pain, his bent and twisted hands gesturing slowly and deliberately as he taught. But I soon learned to focus on what he was saying rather than his physical condition. He seemed to be transformed into another person as he spoke of a life that I knew I needed to experience—the Spirit-filled life. He talked about being filled with the Holy Spirit, the power of the Holy

Spirit, and how God's power could enable me to do whatever God asked of me. He spoke of a spiritual transformation occurring in my heart as the Holy Spirit worked in and through me, making me more and more like Christ if I would only yield my life daily to the work of the Holy Spirit. And what's more, he supported everything he said with Scripture. I wrote down every Bible verse, underlined all of them in my own Bible, and read them again and again. I sensed that these were the secrets to living the life God had in mind for me.

Elmer taught me some of the most important principles I've learned from all my study in God's Word in the past 30 years. His principles about being filled with the Spirit have helped me stand strong in Christ and run my race with the Lord, even during severe trials and tribulations. And these truths about the Holy Spirit and the Spirit-filled life are the secrets to a victorious and abundant Christian life.

I want to share these secrets about the Holy Spirit with you so you can live out God's purpose and plan for your life. You cannot do that without the power of the Holy Spirit. God's plan for you is higher and greater than you can possibly imagine and will involve activities, responsibilities, and difficulties you could never tackle in your own strength. You need His power and His person at work in and through you. The Spirit-filled life is not a lofty ideal; it is the life Christ promised you—it is how He intends for you to live. Jesus said, "I came that they may have life, and have it abundantly" (John 10:10). I want this abundant life for you.

God reveals through Paul in Ephesians 5:18 (NLT) that being filled with the Spirit is a command: "Don't be drunk with wine, because that will ruin your life. Instead, be filled with the Spirit." In Galatians, Paul offers these words about how to live: "So I say, let the Holy Spirit guide your lives. Then you won't be doing what your sinful nature craves" (Galatians 5:16 NLT). He confirms the necessity of the Holy Spirit: "Since we are living by the Spirit, let us follow the Spirit's leading in every part of our lives" (Galatians 5:25 NLT). The Spirit-filled life is more than a whimsical suggestion; it is the normal Christian life described throughout the entire New Testament. You see the results in the early church. In Acts, when people gave their lives to Christ, the old ways became new, and bad people (Saul the persecutor) became good (Paul the apostle).

aused such dramatic changes? One thing only—the work of the Holy Spirit in the hearts of men and women.

Who is the Holy Spirit? What does being filled with the Holy Spirit entail? How can I follow the Holy Spirit's leading in every part of my life? These, my friend, are some of the great questions leading to a deep and abundant life. The Bible's answers are the secrets to experiencing power and victory in your life. They are the secrets to experiencing the great adventure of knowing God.

Why do I call them secrets? Secrets are truths God reveals to those who want to know them, who will draw near to Him and search for them in His Word. God extends this invitation to Jeremiah: "Pray to me and I will answer you. I will tell you important secrets you have never heard before" (Jeremiah 33:3 NCV). The psalmist understood this principle: "Friendship with God is reserved for those who reverence him. With them alone he shares the secrets of his promises" (Psalm 25:14 TLB). In Daniel 2:28 (NLT) we learn that "there is a God in heaven who reveals secrets."

I know that many in the church have not discovered these truths about the Holy Spirit. They rarely open the Bible outside of church; its words are unknown to them—a tragic situation. No wonder the church is in such disarray in many places and blends imperceptibly with the world. Many years ago, as if prophetically, A.W. Tozer offered this assessment:

> The Church has surrendered her once lofty concept of God and has substituted for it one so low, so ignoble, as to be utterly unworthy of thinking, worshiping men. This she has done not deliberately, but little by little and without her knowledge; and her very unawareness only makes her situation all the more tragic.[1]

We remain unaware of magnificent spiritual truths from God when we leave our Bibles unopened, unread, and unstudied.

God offers an incredible treasure for us in His Word. I am compelled to point out the treasure we have within our grasp—the magnificent Spirit-filled life. I am excited to embark on this journey into the Word of God, to discover together with you the secrets contained in the pages of the Bible, and to experience anew the mighty, transforming power of the Holy Spirit. Although I have studied the Bible for many years, I am still learning these secrets from God's Word and applying them to my own life.

You may wonder what you can expect to happen when we discover these secrets and begin applying them in our own lives. Our hearts will catch on fire for Jesus Christ. When I first became a Christian, my new friends pointed to certain men and women and said, "They are on fire for Jesus Christ." I wasn't exactly certain what they meant, but I knew it was a good thing, and I knew I wanted to experience it. I learned later, as I listened to Elmer Lappen, that the Spirit-filled life is a life that is "on fire" for Jesus Christ. And when hearts are on fire for Jesus, the fire spreads everywhere, igniting other hearts in such a way that they are drawn to the Lord—to know Him, to love Him, and to live for Him.

This 30-day journey will empower you to experience God's plan, person, presence, power, and purpose through the mighty work of the Holy Spirit in your heart and life. When you apply what you learn about the Holy Spirit, your heart is going to burn on fire for Jesus Christ, and you will never be the same.

HOW TO USE *SET MY HEART ON FIRE*

Each week you will *read, respond,* and *experience.*

Read. In each day's reading, interact with the ideas by underlining what is significant to you and writing your comments in the margins. This book will encourage you to learn about the Holy Spirit, relate to Him, and experience His power and person in your own life. Please mark this book up, dialogue with what it says, and make it yours! You will also want to keep your Bible close by to look up those verses that mean the most to you on this 30-day journey.

Respond. To help you think through and apply all that is written here, I have included a devotional response section at the end of each day. You'll find a key verse to meditate on and memorize, questions to consider, and a place to express your thoughts and respond to what you have read. This is your opportunity to dialogue with God about the Holy Spirit and His power in your life.

Experience. A complete quiet time at the end of every week emphasizes the principles in that section. Use the blank Notes page to record what you learn from the *Set My Heart on Fire* companion DVD.

Share your journey. Read what others are learning on their journey through *Set My Heart on Fire* and share your own insights with others throughout the world by posting your thoughts on the Quiet Time Ministries discussion board at www.quiettimecafe.com.

SUGGESTED APPROACHES

You can benefit from this book in several ways:

Sequentially. You may want to read the book a day at a time and implement the principles before moving to the next chapter.

Topically. You may have specific topics of interest to you. If that is the case, you can look at the table of contents and focus on those topics.

Devotionally. You may choose to read this book over 30 days. The days are divided into five sections so you can take five weeks to read and think about the Spirit-filled life. It can be a 30-day adventure!

SUGGESTED SETTINGS

Personal and private. This is the kind of book you can read again and again. It will encourage you to draw near to God, especially if you have lost a habit of spending time with your Lord in His Word or you need to shake up your quiet time because it has become lackluster and routine. You might even want to invest some extended time with this book in a beautiful setting to revive and refresh your relationship with the Lord. It's a retreat in a book!

Small groups. I encourage you to travel on this 30-day journey with some friends. Sharing what you are learning with others who also love the Lord brings tremendous joy. Use the questions at the end of each day for your discussion together. More discussion questions are in Appendix 1. This book may be used in Sunday school classes, Bible study groups, church congregations, or your family devotions.

Ministry revival campaign. You may also desire to use this book as a 30-day intensive campaign to teach, revive, and inspire those in your ministry in the area of spiritual growth and the Spirit-filled life. Using it as a campaign will help grow your ministry as new small groups are formed. Six accompanying messages on DVD are available from Quiet Time Ministries. For more information about how to use this book as a spiritual growth campaign for your group, visit www.30dayjourney.com or www.setmyheartonfire.com.

Now let's engage in this amazing journey! This book is my conversation with you about how to experience the power of the Holy Spirit in your own life. I want you to look at these 30 days as some of the most important you will ever experience. Here is the challenge before us: Are we willing to step out of the crowd and choose to be numbered with those who live by what God says in His Word? Will we be so sold out to Jesus Christ that we will often appear reckless in our faith, choosing to trust God instead of living in the gray twilight of compromise and complacency?

You may be thinking, *I can't live like that.* And I would say you're right. The magnificent truth is that you can't, but He can! Being filled with the Holy Spirit means His power is at work in and through you, enabling you to do what you could never do in your own strength. As you embark on this 30-day journey, may your prayer be, *Lord, set my heart on fire!*

Week One

GOD HAS A
PLAN FOR YOU

Days 1–6

ON THE EMMAUS ROAD

They said to one another, "Were not our hearts burning within us while He was speaking to us on the road, while He was explaining the Scriptures to us?"

LUKE 24:32

Your heart will catch on fire when you meet Jesus on your road to Emmaus. Long ago in ancient Israel, two shocked and desperate men experienced "hearts on fire" when they met a mysterious stranger on the road home from Jerusalem to Emmaus. When they finally realized the stranger was Jesus, they said to one another, "Were not our hearts burning within us while He was speaking to us on the road, while He was explaining the Scriptures to us?" (Luke 24:32). When your heart is dry, downcast, or in despair, the conditions are just right to ignite your heart on fire with the transforming power of the Holy Spirit. When the Word of God confronts even the driest of hearts and the good, strong wind of the Holy Spirit blows, that heart is set on fire. And oh, how that fire can spread to others both near and far away.

Luke describes these two men, downcast and in despair, trudging along the road back to Emmaus, still shaken from the horrific events of previous days. After all, the one they hoped was the Messiah, Jesus of Nazareth, had been arrested, convicted, and crucified like a common criminal. One can imagine their voices low and lifeless, their hearts devastated, and their hopes dashed. But as they were walking along in muted conversation, they met a stranger who began traveling with them, listening to their words.

After a while, this stranger asked them, "What are these words?" In essence, what are you talking about? Luke tells us that "They stood still, looking sad" (Luke 24:17). My guess is that they were literally stopped in their tracks, shocked at the apparent ignorance of their inquirer. One of them, Cleopas, answered in disbelief, "Are You the only one visiting Jerusalem and unaware of the things which have happened here in these days?" When the stranger responded, "What things?" this apparently unleashed the floodgates of pent-up emotions, allowing the two men to bare their souls. They told of the crucifixion of Jesus and the discovery of the empty tomb and missing body. Can you imagine the two hurrying to finish each others' sentences? The words probably couldn't come out fast enough.

When they were finished, their emotions spent, this stranger responded, "O foolish men and slow of heart to believe in all that the prophets have spoken! Was it not necessary for the Christ to suffer these things and to enter into His glory?" Then, the stranger began with Moses and with all the prophets, and "explained to them the things concerning Himself in all the Scriptures" (Luke 24:27).

When they arrived at Emmaus, the two men invited this stranger to stay with them. He went in to their house, and as Luke explains, "reclined at the table with them." As they ate together, the eyes of these two men were opened, and they recognized that the stranger was Jesus Himself. Then, thinking back, they exclaimed, "Were not our hearts burning within us while He was speaking to us on the road, while He was explaining the Scriptures to us?" (Luke 24:32). Once their hearts were set on fire, these two men became powerful witnesses for Jesus Christ. Luke tells us they got up immediately, returned to Jerusalem, and told everyone who was gathered with the 11 disciples that Jesus was indeed risen and that He had spoken with them.

I want to encourage you that Jesus is setting hearts on fire even today. Those whose hearts burn for Him become powerful witnesses of all He has done in their lives. He meets you on your own "road to Emmaus" with a heart ready for a good fire—perhaps dry from the busyness of life or in despair because of a great loss or the dashing of a dream. First, He invites you to an intimate relationship with Him and offers you forgiveness of sins and eternal life. He can make such an offer because He paid the penalty for all your sins by giving His own life in your place on the cross (Romans 5:8).

Once you have received Christ into your life, you are born again spiritually, and you become a new person. "The old life is gone; a new life has begun!" (2 Corinthians 5:17-18 NLT). When you are born again spiritually, "the Spirit of God dwells in you" (Romans 8:9). Because you are now indwelt by the Spirit of God, you are commanded to yield control to Him through the filling of the Holy Spirit on a continual, moment by moment basis: "Be filled with the Holy Spirit" (Ephesians 5:18). Indwelling provides the opportunity for continual filling, making possible the power and presence of Christ in you (Ephesians 3:16-17). This is the supernatural progression leading to a heart on fire.

What is your personal "road to Emmaus"? Perhaps you, like Cleopas and his friend, are disillusioned, and your life has not turned out the way you thought it would. Or perhaps you are wondering how you are going to handle your present stressful position in life. The Lord Jesus would like to meet you on your own road to Emmaus just as He did those two forlorn individuals. Will you open the Bible, the very Word of God, and allow Him to speak with you?

If you are willing, you are already beginning to experience the power of the Holy Spirit for yourself. The Holy Spirit draws you to the Word of God; Jesus wants to speak to you even now in His Word. Jesus said to His disciples while still with them, "There is so much more I want to tell you, but you can't bear it now. When the Spirit of truth comes, he will guide you into all truth. He will not be presenting his own ideas; he will be telling you what he has heard. He will tell you about the future. He will bring me glory by telling you whatever he receives from me" (John 16:12-14 NLT). Jesus will explain the Scriptures to you even now through the work of the Holy Spirit in your life.

One of my heroes of the faith is D.L. Moody, the great American evangelist of the late 1800s. On a recent speaking trip to Chicago, I had an opportunity to visit the school he founded—Moody Bible Institute, now nestled among tall steel and glass structures of corporate America. While at the institute, I explored the Moody archives, looked at some of the hundreds of Moody's sermons, and actually handled his lecture notes for myself. I saw perhaps a dozen file cabinets filled with messages and letters of this prolific writer, preacher, and evangelist.

This was a humbling but inspiring experience for me as an author. Moody was a man of unassuming appearance, largely unschooled, and yet God used him in a powerful way. God gave Moody the great opportunity to preach to more than a million people in his lifetime. Thousands put their trust in Christ because of him; many more have learned about Christ and prepared for ministry by attending Moody Bible Institute. How could this one man have such an impact on the world for Jesus Christ? Moody had learned the secret to a Spirit-filled life. And that secret yielded powerful results.

Early on in his Christian experience, Moody visited Charles Spurgeon's church in England. Spurgeon, mind you, was so popular that a ticket was required to attend one of his services at the Metropolitan Tabernacle. On the day of the visit, Moody was barred from entry by an usher. Ever zealous, determined, and resourceful, Moody borrowed skills from his persuasive days as a shoe salesman and argued his way into the service. Here is the secret Moody learned, best understood from his own words following his time at Spurgeon's church:

> But let me just say this, if God can use Mr. Spurgeon why not the rest of us, and why should not we all just lay ourselves at the Master's feet, and say "Send me, use me"? It is not Mr. Spurgeon after all, it is God. He is as weak as any other man away from Him. Moses was nothing, but it was Moses' God. Samson was nothing when he lost his strength, but when it came back to him then he was a mighty man; and so, dear friends, bear in mind that if we can just link our weakness to God's strength we can go forth and be a blessing in the world.[1]

God intends to set each of our hearts on fire and spread His love to those around us. The secret is in what Moody says: We need to "link our weakness to God's strength." What is the source of God's strength for your life? The Holy Spirit. The more your heart burns for Jesus, the more others will see the light of His love and be drawn to Him. "But thanks be to God, who always leads us in triumph in Christ, and manifests through us the sweet aroma of the knowledge of Him in every place. For we are a fragrance of Christ to God among those who are being saved and among those who are perishing" (2 Corinthians 2:14-15). We cannot command or control the movement of the Holy Spirit. May you and I have hearts that catch on fire and burn brightly for Jesus Christ.

Oh, what a life the Lord has in store for you as you engage in a relationship with Him. This abundant life is God's plan designed just for you. What is the secret to this kind of life that occurs when Jesus meets a lonely soul on his or her road to Emmaus? The secret is found in the person of the Holy Spirit: who He is and what He does. And so, as we begin this journey together, take some time now and pray, *Lord, set my heart on fire.*

My Response

DATE:

KEY VERSE: "They said to one another, 'Were not our hearts burning within us while He was speaking to us on the road, while He was explaining the Scriptures to us?'" (Luke 24:32).

FOR FURTHER THOUGHT: At the outset of this journey and as you think about meeting Jesus, do you have a personal relationship with Him? If not, will you make a decision now to ask Him to come into your life? You may pray a prayer like this: *Lord Jesus, I need You. Thank you for dying on the cross for my sins. I ask You now to come into my life, forgive my sins, give me eternal life, and make me the person You want me to be, in Jesus' name. Amen.* If you prayed that prayer for the first time, you can know that Jesus is living in you, and you have been "born again to a living hope" (1 Peter 1:3) and are now indwelt by the Holy Spirit (Romans 8:9).

What are you facing on your Emmaus road today? Is it something that seems impossible? You can know that Jesus will indeed meet with you right where you are, and what is impossible to you is made possible through Him. Always remember, "you can't, but He can." Will you draw near to Him and fellowship with Him? Oh, may He give you, as a result of your time with Him in His Word, a heart on fire.

As you begin this 30-day journey, take some time now to talk with the Lord about where you are and what you hope to gain from your time with Him. Write a prayer to Him in the form of a letter in the space provided and then watch what He does in your life over the next 30 days.

MY RESPONSE: A Letter to the Lord

Day Two

WHEN YOUR HEART CATCHES FIRE

*You will receive power when the Holy
Spirit has come upon you; and you shall
be My witnesses both in Jerusalem, and
in all Judea and Samaria, and even
to the remotest part of the earth.*

ACTS 1:8

Y ou will experience the power of God in your life when your heart
catches fire with the Holy Spirit. His power enables you to be His
witness throughout the world, accomplishing a mission you cannot carry
out in your own strength. Jesus promised the Holy Spirit to His disciples
just prior to His ascension to heaven, emphasizing the Holy Spirit's vital
importance to their lives and ministry. Jesus promised, "You will receive
power when the Holy Spirit has come upon you; and you shall be My
witnesses both in Jerusalem, and in all Judea and Samaria, and even to
the remotest part of the earth" (Acts 1:8).

The Greek word *dunamis,* translated "power" in Acts 1:8, gives us the
word *dynamite* and points to a power that can make you able, capable,
and achieving. Jesus is saying that the Holy Spirit will give you an ability

you do not naturally possess. We see the demonstration of this supernatural power in the lives of the disciples throughout the book of Acts. When comparing the Gospels with the book of Acts, you will notice that something powerful and dynamic must have happened between those two accounts because the disciples demonstrated a dramatic change in how they spoke and lived. That something was the outpouring of the Holy Spirit on Pentecost, described in the second chapter of Acts. This outpouring of the Holy Spirit was the fulfillment of the promise God gave through the prophet Joel many centuries earlier: "It will come about after this that I will pour out My Spirit on all mankind; and your sons and daughters will prophesy, your old men will dream dreams, your young men will see visions. And even on the male and female servants I will pour out My Spirit in those days" (Joel 2:28-29).

Luke begins this pivotal chapter in church history, Acts 2, with the words "When the day of Pentecost had come..." The word *Pentecost* comes from the Greek word *pentecoste,* which means "fiftieth." The Jews celebrated Pentecost as the Feast of Harvest (Exodus 23:16) on the fiftieth day after Passover, presenting the firstfruits of the wheat harvest to God. How fitting that God would choose the day of Pentecost, celebrating a physical harvest, to empower His disciples for the upcoming spiritual harvest!

Upon Jesus' command of Acts 1:4, the disciples were waiting together in Jerusalem to be baptized with the Holy Spirit. "And suddenly there came from heaven a noise like a violent rushing wind, and it filled the whole house where they were sitting...And they were all filled with the Holy Spirit" (Acts 2:2-4). What happened next was more than amazing; it was miraculous. Luke records that the disciples "began to speak with other tongues, as the Spirit was giving them utterance." Jews from every nation heard the disciples speaking in their own languages: Parthians, Medes, Elamites, and people from Mesopotamia, Judea, Cappadocia, Pontus, Asia, Phrygia, Pamphylia, Egypt, Libya, Rome, Crete, and Arabia. Remember that the disciples of Jesus were simple men who served God and had not been experts in linguistics or translation. The list of languages is extensive and emphasizes Luke's amazement at this first act of the Holy Spirit in the lives of the disciples, enabling them to become witnesses to all nations.

The fact that the disciples were speaking languages from other parts of the world was a powerful witness to a supernatural work of God. Some in the crowd accused the disciples of being drunk. Peter, "taking his stand with the eleven, raised his voice," and preached a bold, confident, and powerful sermon, far beyond his talents as a simple fisherman. He masterfully wove Scripture from the Old Testament into an apologetic defense of the deity of Christ. Those who heard were, as the Scripture says, "pierced to the heart" and moved to a point of decision for Christ. They asked Peter and the other apostles, "Brethren, what shall we do?"

Peter responded, "Repent, and each of you be baptized in the name of Jesus Christ for the forgiveness of your sins; and you will receive the gift of the Holy Spirit" (Acts 2:38).

About three thousand people experienced salvation that day—evidence of an amazing power, the *dunamis* of the Holy Spirit at work in the lives of simple, uneducated men. Jesus' disciples were no longer the timid and fearful men who ran away when Jesus was arrested, but bold and courageous, willing to live for Him in the midst of a godless world. Rather than running away they boldly stood strong for Jesus, and most of them ultimately died a martyr's death.

Perhaps you are thinking, *Yes, but those were the disciples who walked with Jesus. God could never do those kinds of things through me. And besides, I am facing unbelievable adversity and enduring painful affliction. I am completely without resources to accomplish anything for the Lord.* You need to know that the less you can do, the more God's power can accomplish. Paul learned this secret when God told him, "Power is perfected in weakness" (2 Corinthians 12:9). The weaker you are, the better God's power can perform. That means when you are down and defeat appears imminent, you are actually on the verge of victory. Despite what the world says, even when you are down, you are never out. When things are at their worst, God has something He wants to do in and through you. Even if you are really down and desperate, God's infinite power can accomplish the seemingly impossible—God's plan in God's way in God's time and in God's extraordinary, supernatural power.

God's plan for you will involve the difficult, the painful, and even the improbable. But always remember, God is not counting on your limited strength and resources but on His own power and sufficiency. The secret is to run to God and depend on the power of the Holy Spirit. "Not that we are adequate in ourselves to consider anything as coming from ourselves, but our adequacy is from God" (2 Corinthians 3:5). Discount your own strength and resources as utterly insufficient when compared to the mighty power of God.

Paul suffered from a malady that made his life and ministry difficult. Scripture does not identify Paul's affliction. Perhaps it is better that we do not know so we can use our imaginations and readily identify with Paul. We do know that Paul hated this thorn in the flesh so much that he begged God three times to take it away from him. The Lord answered Paul this way: "My grace is sufficient for you, for power is perfected in weakness" (2 Corinthians 12:9). Paul called it a "thorn in the flesh" and a "messenger of Satan" (2 Corinthians 12:7), but God interpreted Paul's situation as weakness.

No one likes to be called weak—at least not in this "survival of the fittest" world. But in God's economy, weakness is a plus, a bonus, and grounds to boast. In the spiritual realm, you can shout from the mountaintop or from the deepest valley for all to hear, "I am weak!" That is basically what Paul taught the Corinthian church. He possessed every earthly qualification for success and greatness in his day: the best lineage, the best intellect, and the best academic training. From the world's viewpoint, Paul could do just about anything in his own strength. However, Paul learned from God that the greatest weakness is better than the greatest strength. He was able to exclaim, "Most gladly, therefore, I will rather boast about my weaknesses, so that the power of Christ may dwell in me...content with weaknesses, with insults, with distresses, with persecutions, with difficulties, for Christ's sake; for when I am weak, then I am strong" (2 Corinthians 12:9-10).

There is your battle cry, my friend. "When I am weak, then I am strong!" That is not the world's point of view; that is God's point of view. The Greek word translated "strong" is *dunatos* and means "able." Your weakness may deceive you into thinking you cannot handle your particular challenge or distress. But God is assuring you that in His economy, your weakness qualifies you for His strength and power to accomplish what faces you today. He gives you a new claim in your weakness: "I am able! I can—in His power!" That's why Paul was able to say, "I can do all things through Him who strengthens me" (Philippians 4:13).

God can accomplish what is humanly impossible. God revealed Himself to Abraham as *El Shaddai*, Almighty God, when He promised him innumerable descendants. The Lord said to Abraham, "Is anything too difficult for the LORD?" (Genesis 18:14). Jeremiah, overwhelmed by the creation of the heavens and the earth, exclaimed, "Nothing is too difficult for You" (Jeremiah 32:17). Even Job, following his trials and tribulations, reverently acknowledged, "I know that You can do all things, and that no purpose of Yours can be thwarted" (Job 42:2). Paul believed God for the impossible in his classic benediction, "Now to him who is able to do immeasurably more than all we ask or imagine, according to his power that is at work within us..." (Ephesians 3:20 NIV). And so, dear friend, how should you respond in your weakness when you face a trial? You must depend on God—actively, not passively—relying on the truth of God's Word and acting on the promises of God regardless of the depth of your weakness or the extent of your incapability.

Weakness qualifies you for service in the kingdom of God. Perhaps that is why Charles Spurgeon accomplished so much in his life. He had a practice of reading six books a week. He wrote and preached thousands of sermons, published thousands of articles and dozens of books and letters (without a computer), founded schools, and pastored a church. He suffered illness and devastating bouts of depression. Spurgeon punctuates the importance of weakness in this passage from his devotional *Morning and Evening:*

> A primary qualification for serving God with any amount of success, and for doing God's work well and triumphantly, is a sense of our own weakness. When God's warrior marches forth to battle, strong in his own might, when he boasts, "I know that I shall conquer, my own right arm and my conquering sword shall get unto me the victory," defeat is not far distant. God will not go forth with that man who marches in his own strength. He who reckoneth on victory thus has reckoned wrongly, for "it is not by might, nor by power, but by my Spirit, saith the Lord of hosts" (Zechariah 4:6)... God will have no strength used in His battles but

the strength which He Himself imparts. Are you mourning over your own weakness? Take courage, for there must be a consciousness of weakness before the Lord will give thee victory. Your emptiness is but the preparation for your being filled, and your casting down is but the making ready for your lifting up.[1]

Men and women through the centuries have been able to accomplish more than they could have imagined because the power of the Holy Spirit was at work in their lives. In this generation we need Spirit-filled believers with hearts on fire who are willing to step beyond the boundaries of their own abilities. We need believers who dare to do great and mighty works in the name of Christ and in His power as He leads them in life. Instead of living by fear, we must live by faith in what God says in His Word. Instead of falling into despair, we must engage in hope in the promises of God. Instead of worrying in our circumstances, we must be bold and courageous in the power of God. Perhaps you will resolve to be one of the weak ones who hold to the promise of God for His power perfected in weakness, declaring with Paul, "When I am weak, then I am strong!" and adding, "I can't, but He can!"

My Response

DATE:

KEY VERSE: "You will receive power when the Holy Spirit has come upon you; and you shall be My witnesses both in Jerusalem, and in all Judea and Samaria, and even to the remotest part of the earth" (Acts 1:8).

FOR FURTHER THOUGHT: Have you experienced the power of the Holy Spirit in your own life, enabling you to do what you were unable to do in your own strength? Where in your life are you weak and in need of the power of the Holy Spirit? Will you ask Him to empower you today? Write your response in the space provided.

MY RESPONSE:

RUN BEFORE
THE WIND

*Don't be drunk with wine, because
that will ruin your life. Instead,
be filled with the Holy Spirit.*

Ephesians 5:18 nlt

≫

God wants to empower you through the filling of the Holy Spirit. Indeed, He commands us to be filled with the Holy Spirit: "Don't be drunk with wine, because that will ruin your life. Instead, be filled with the Holy Spirit" (Ephesians 5:18 nlt). Paul was speaking to believers in the Ephesian church. All Christians are baptized (1 Corinthians 12:13) and indwelt (Romans 8:9) by the Spirit of God. That is the "born again" salvation experience Jesus described to Nicodemus: "Unless one is born of water and the Spirit he cannot enter into the kingdom of God" (John 3:5). All Christians are baptized and indwelt by the Holy Spirit, but not all Christians yield to His control and empowerment—not all Christians are filled with the Holy Spirit.

The day of Pentecost ushered in a new era for the church involving the *permanent* residence of the Holy Spirit in the life of the believer.

This was an unprecedented, transitory period in history. Kistemaker and Hendriksen, in their commentary on Acts, support this view.[1] J. Montgomery Boice leans toward Pentecost as a filling of the Holy Spirit to those who were already believers, rather than baptism or indwelling. Lewis Sperry Chafer, in his classic study on spirituality, *He That Is Spiritual,* seems to take the position that indwelling, baptism, and filling of the Holy Spirit need not be viewed as mutually exclusive events on the day of Pentecost.[2] Academic controversy aside, my emphasis is rather on the Pauline command, "Be filled with the Spirit" (Ephesians 5:18).

On the day of Pentecost, the Holy Spirit came as a "violent rushing wind" (Acts 2:2). The Holy Spirit is like a wind that often blows in unpredictable directions. You can't plan His moves. You can't command Him, and you can't control Him. When you are filled with the Holy Spirit, He controls you. The Greek word translated "filled" is *pleroo* and means "to fill to the brim and overflowing." *Pleroo* is a verb with continuous action—we are to keep on being filled with the Holy Spirit. Once filled, a believer must be filled again and again.

When the Holy Spirit works in your life, He is like a wind in your sails, moving you in His desired direction. When He worked in the lives of those He used as instruments to inspire the Bible, the Word of God, He moved them to write. Peter says in 2 Peter 1:20-21 (NIV), "Above all, you must understand that no prophecy of Scripture came about by the prophet's own interpretation. For prophecy never had its origin in the will of man, but men spoke from God as they were carried along by the Holy Spirit." The Greek word translated "carried along" is *phero* and means to bear, carry, or bring along. It was used of a ship carried along by the wind, as we see in Acts 27:17. In 2 Peter 1:21, the metaphor is picturing prophets "raising their sails, the Holy Spirit filling them and carrying their craft along in the direction He wished."[3] Indeed, the Lord desires to move the craft of your life in the power of His Holy Spirit, filling your sails and empowering you to glide freely and powerfully on the ocean of His love.

When you are filled with the Holy Spirit, the wind of the Spirit moves in the direction of God's plan for your life. Chafer says, "To be filled with the Spirit is to have the Spirit fulfilling in us all that God intended Him to do when He placed Him there."[4] This filling brings the sense of completeness and wholeness. Dr. Bill Bright, founder of Campus Crusade for Christ, says, "To be filled with the Holy Spirit is to be filled with Christ and to be abiding in Him…Through His indwelling presence, He wants to enable all who will place their trust in Him to live this same supernatural life."[5] This establishes a sense of identity. Finally, A.B. Simpson describes the filling of the Holy Spirit with this summary:

> It does not mean to have only a measure of the Holy Spirit, but to be wholly filled with and possessed by the Holy Ghost—to be utterly lost in the life and fullness of Jesus… All is connected with a living Person. We are not filled with an influence; we are not filled with a sensation; we are not filled with a set of ideas and truths; we are not filled with a blessing—we are filled with a Person. Christianity centers in a living Person and its very essence is the indwelling life of Christ Himself. This Person is the true fullness of *every* part of our life.[6]

This quote reveals a sense of abandonment to the will of God. The filling of the Holy Spirit is never about how much you have of the Holy Spirit, but how much He has of you. The focus is what God does in and through you, not what you do for God. He is the wind in your sails, and He enables you to launch out on the ocean of His love and run before the wind.

Have you ever watched a sailboat whose sails are in the perfect position to catch the wind? The sailboat moves so fast and smooth that it seems to glide effortlessly on the water. Many years ago, my husband and I ventured out on a sunset cruise off the west coast of Maui in Hawaii. I had never been on a sailboat before, and I had no idea what to expect. Our captain was a young man in his twenties whose obvious love of sailing allayed my fears. Once away from the dock, he maneuvered the sailboat and the sails one way and then another. Suddenly, the sails caught the direction and movement of the wind, and we jolted forward, slicing across the azure water with ever-increasing speed. The captain shouted with pleasure as the wind blew through his hair and our boat effortlessly ran before the wind.

When we are filled with the Spirit of God, we are like that sailboat, enabled to run before the wind of God's purposeful action in our own life. We are no longer in control—He is in control. We are no longer in power—He is the power in our life. He ignites a fire in our hearts. As the wind of the Holy Spirit continues to blow through our lives, the fire continues to grow.

That's how revivals begin and grow with force, starting with a spark in the heart of one person who turns to the Lord and asks to be filled with the Holy Spirit. Oh, what a fire began in Wales that day in 1904 when young Evan Roberts heard a speaker pray for his congregation, "Lord, bend us." On the spot, Roberts decided it was a prayer he needed to pray for himself. He ran to the front of the room and cried out, "Lord, bend *me!*" That was the beginning of the Welsh Revival of 1904–1905, and all of Wales was soon like one gigantic prayer meeting.

Forest fires move with force and power even though they begin with only a single spark. Several years ago, some fires started by a spark at a campground devastated portions of drought-ridden Arizona. My husband and I saw one of those fires close at hand as we were staying at a hotel just outside of Phoenix. On the afternoon of our arrival, we could see smoke in the distance coming from the other side of the adjacent mountain range, but no flames. Later that evening, as we were sitting in our room watching television, I happened to look out the window and gasped with horror. Huge red flames were roaring skyward from the tops of the mountains immediately next to our hotel—a spark away from reaching us. Needless to say, we packed up our belongings and checked out within the hour, moving to a hotel farther away. We had learned just how fast a fire can move when the wind is blowing.

The same is true when you are filled with the Holy Spirit. God will move in and through your life, empowering you and touching the lives of others in ways you could never have imagined—with power and force.

I remember when I met my friend Myra for the first time. She had a sparkle in her eyes as she introduced herself at our church's women's ministries table. A few minutes later, pleasantries aside, she lowered her voice, stared me straight in the eyes, and confided, "Catherine, I'll do anything in your ministry—just don't ever ask me to get up in front of a group to speak."

I looked at her and smiled, knowing that with the Lord you can never say what you will or will not do. Months later, I handed the microphone to Myra and asked her to announce an upcoming women's revival conference.

She said, "Catherine, I would never do this by my own design, but for the Lord, I'll do it. I want to see women come to our conference."

Well, you can guess what happened next. Filled with the Holy Spirit, Myra began speaking, and I didn't know if I was ever going to get the microphone back. Myra has now become an eloquent speaker for Christian Women's Club and a diligent teacher of the Word of God. Myra is an example of what God can accomplish in and through someone who allows the Holy Spirit to fill them, someone who says yes to the Lord.

To run before the wind is to live the Spirit-filled life. How can you be filled with the Holy Spirit? The filling of the Holy Spirit involves four actions on your part that will help you appropriate His power in your life:

Confess your sins to God. God does not fill unclean vessels. When He convicts you of a transgression, confess it—agree with God that you have sinned. John says, "If we confess our sins, He is faithful and righteous to forgive us our sins and to cleanse us from all unrighteousness" (1 John 1:9).

Surrender yourself to God. God wants all of you with nothing held back. In this act of surrender, you give way to God's ways. Paul says, "Therefore I urge you, brethren, by the mercies of God, to present your bodies a living and holy sacrifice, acceptable to God, which is your spiritual service of worship" (Romans 12:1). If you are struggling with surrender in any area of your life, pray, *Lord, I'm willing to be made willing.*

Pray to be filled with the Holy Spirit. Simply respond to God's command and ask Him to fill you, to control and empower you. We've seen that Paul issues this command in Ephesians 5:18: "Be filled with the Holy Spirit." You can trust that God has answered your prayer, for He promises in 1 John 5:14-15, "If we ask anything according to His will, He hears us. And if we know that He hears us in whatever we ask, we know that we have the requests which we have asked from Him."

Faithfully follow the lead of the Holy Spirit in every part of your life. The filling of the Holy Spirit is not a once and for all act, but a continuous, ongoing, moment by moment process. Andrew Murray describes the continuing need for the Holy Spirit's power this way: "Our lungs are full of breath, yet call for a fresh supply every moment; our fingers pulse with the fullness of blood, yet continually call to the heart for a fresh supply. We should praise God for the Spirit that has been received, and yet always desire His fuller inflow."[7] Paul says, "Since we live by the Spirit, let us keep in step with the Spirit" (Galatians 5:25 NIV). The New Living Translation renders this verse, "Since we are living by the Spirit, let us follow the Spirit's leading in every part of our lives." When we keep in step with the Spirit, we must be continually alert to follow His lead. If we sin, we must confess our sin. If He takes us in a new direction, rather than wrestling with Him, we must come to the place of surrender and say, "Yes, Lord." We will need to adjust our lives to His moves in our life.

These four actions of confession, surrender, prayer, and faithful following are the means of appropriating all that the Holy Spirit is and does in your life. In the weeks to come you are going to learn more about the person and work of the Holy Spirit. You need His power, and God is more than willing to give you what you need.

What happens when you are filled with the Holy Spirit? Your life will exhibit the fruit of the Holy Spirit, the character of Christ: His love, joy, peace, patience, kindness, goodness, faithfulness, gentleness, and self-control (Galatians 5:22-23). Jesus will live His life in and through you (Galatians 2:20). You will have pure motives and will desire to do the will of God and accomplish His work (John 4:34). You will experience an abundant, overflowing life (John 7:37-39). You will experience supernatural power in your life—power to witness, serve God, and engage in spiritual warfare (Acts 1:8; Philippians 4:13; John 14:12; Ephesians 6:10-20). You will experience God's comfort and help even when earthly hope seems gone (John 14:16; Acts 9:31; 2 Corinthians 1:3-5). You will experience a supernatural contentment even when you are in dire circumstances (Philippians 4:11). You will grow in your devotion to prayer and intercession (Romans 8:26-27; Philippians 4:6-7; 1 Thessalonians 5:17). You will grow in your knowledge and understanding of what God says in His Word, the Bible (John 14:26; 1 Corinthians 2:9-13).

Throughout this book, you will see that the Holy Spirit changes the face of everything in your life—He gives you the life you are meant to live. One of my favorite writers, John Henry Jowett, summarizes the filling of the Holy Spirit this way: "He adds sunshine to daylight. He transmutes happiness into blessedness. He endows our delights with heavenly virtue…When the Great Spirit broods over our business it becomes our Father's business…the faithful Spirit broods upon the waters and the soul is kept in perfect peace."[8]

Perhaps you know the story of the Texas rancher and the eagle. The rancher, hunting in the mountains, came upon an eagle's nest and took one of the eggs back home with him, placing it under a setting hen. The eagle was hatched and cared for by the mother hen. For some period of time, the eagle seemed perfectly content to remain in the barnyard and feed along with the chickens. But one day, it heard the harsh scream of a mature eagle, swooping down in search of prey. In the blink of an eye, the young eagle ascended into the sky and was never seen again. He had found his new home in the mountainside cliffs, for he was not made for the barnyard dirt.

Dear friend, do you see that the Spirit-filled life is the life God designed for you? Jesus was full of the Spirit (Luke 4:1); Zacharias, Elizabeth, and John were filled with the Spirit (Luke 1:15,41,67); the disciples and others were filled again and again with the Holy Spirit (Acts 2:4; 4:8,31; 6:3; 7:55; 9:17; 11:24; 13:52); and you must be filled with the Holy Spirit (Ephesians 5:18). When you keep in step with the Spirit of God, following His lead and walking intimately with the Lord Jesus Christ, you will have just a taste, a glimpse, of life in the eternal kingdom of God where you will be face-to-face with Jesus.

You are not made to live in the barnyard dirt of this world. You are not meant to walk in the mire of darkness, to plod along in despair, to wrestle meekly in the morass of sin and temptation. You are meant to fly with wings like an eagle and soar with the wind of the Holy Spirit. Jowett affirms Isaiah 40:28-31 when he says, "We are the birds of God, endowed with power to mount up with wings as eagles, to respond to the upward calling, and to breathe the lofty air of the heavenliness in Christ Jesus."[9]

Will you ask God to fill you with His Holy Spirit today? Will you experience the rushing wind in your sails? Will you run before the wind?

Perhaps you will be the catalyst for something amazing and wonderful that God wants to do in your time and in your generation.

Lord God, the heavens rend,
Come down and set us free:
A great revival send—
Begin the work in me.

Remove the veil of sin
That separates from Thee:
Lord, search our hearts within—
Begin the work in me.

The cleansing Blood we plead;
We claim the victory:
Thou canst supply our need—
Begin the work in me.

Our humble prayer attend,
Revival comes from Thee,
O Holy Ghost descend—
Begin the work in me.[10]

J. EDWIN ORR

My Response

DATE:

KEY VERSE: "Don't be drunk with wine, because that will ruin your life. Instead, be filled with the Holy Spirit" (Ephesians 5:18 NLT).

FOR FURTHER THOUGHT: Write out in your own words the meaning of being filled with the Holy Spirit. Why should every Christian be filled with the Holy Spirit? What can happen as a result? Close by writing a prayer to the Lord and include the four actions involved in being filled with the Holy Spirit.

MY RESPONSE:

Day Four

SETTING YOUR SAIL

*Therefore I urge you, brethren, by the
mercies of God, to present your bodies
a living and holy sacrifice, acceptable to
God, which is your spiritual service of
worship. And do not be conformed to
this world, but be transformed by the
renewing of your mind, so that you may
prove what the will of God is, that which
is good and acceptable and perfect.*

ROMANS 12:1-2

S urrender is the key to the Spirit-filled life. Surrender to God sets you apart for God, gives Christ control of your life, and helps you experience His ways and His purposes for you. This is "setting your sail" to run before the wind of the Holy Spirit. Your life is not meant to be merely an imitation of Jesus but a complete surrender to the person of Christ living in you and through you.

How is such a dramatic surrender possible? Paul says, "Therefore I urge you, brethren, by the mercies of God, to present your bodies a living and holy sacrifice, acceptable to God, which is your spiritual service of worship. And do not be conformed to this world, but be transformed by the renewing of your mind, so that you may prove what the will of God is, that which is good and acceptable and perfect" (Romans 12:1-2).

The nautical term *to bear away* means "to change the course of a ship so she can run before the wind." When you set your sail, moving it to a new position where it can catch the wind, you present yourself to Christ in surrender to Him and literally change the course of your life so you can run before the wind of the Holy Spirit as He moves in your life. This surrender is probably the most difficult aspect of appropriating the power of the Holy Spirit and yet results in God's most dramatic activities in and through you. A.B. Simpson explains, "The Holy Spirit is especially sensitive to the reception He finds in the human heart; never intruding as an unwelcome guest, but gladly entering every open door, and following up every invitation with His faithful love and power."[1] Setting your sail opens the door to the Holy Spirit.

Have you noticed that not all Christians live the way Christ lived? Not all believers set their sails, catch the wind, and are filled with the Holy Spirit. A struggle takes place in every believer—the struggle between the flesh and the Spirit. Paul describes it this way: "For the good that I want, I do not do, but I practice the very evil that I do not want" (Romans 7:19). In 1 Corinthians 3:1-3, Paul describes the two kinds of Christians as "spiritual men" and "men of flesh." One is able to eat the "solid food" of the Word of God, and the other is still an infant drinking milk.

We see this same distinction between the flesh and the Spirit in Paul's letter to the Galatians. He says that the deeds of the flesh are evident: "immorality, impurity, sensuality, idolatry, sorcery, enmities, strife, jealousy, outbursts of anger, disputes, dissensions, factions, envying, drunkenness, carousing, and things like these" (Galatians 5:19-21). Then Paul contrasts these with the fruit of the Spirit: "love, joy, peace, patience, kindness, goodness, faithfulness, gentleness, self-control; against such things there is no law" (Galatians 5:22-23).

What then is the secret to displaying the fruit of the Spirit (spiritual Christian living) instead of the deeds of the flesh (carnal Christian living)? Paul gives us the answer in Galatians 5:16: "But I say, walk by the Spirit, and you will not carry out the desire of the flesh." And what is the secret to saying yes to the Spirit and no to the flesh? Paul points to our union with Christ in His death, burial, and resurrection in Galatians 5:24: "Now those who belong to Christ Jesus have crucified the flesh with its passions and desires."

Because of the work of God in me (union with Christ) and the indwelling Spirit, I can do something I was incapable of doing before I became a Christian. Now I have the Holy Spirit's indwelling power to say yes to God, to say no to sin, and to present myself to Him, saying, "Here I am, Lord, use me as You desire." This does not mean we will never sin again because we are in our fleshly bodies here on earth. However, our life is not meant to be (and does not need to be) characterized by habitual sin. Peter encourages believers in this regard by saying, "Beloved, I urge you as aliens and strangers to abstain from fleshly lusts which wage war against the soul. Keep your behavior excellent" (1 Peter 2:11).

Moving from the life of a fleshly Christian to become a spiritual man or woman of God is the process of sanctification and is brought about by the work of the Holy Spirit in your heart. Peter points out that the work of the Holy Spirit is a "sanctifying work" (1 Peter 1:2). The Greek word translated "sanctification" is *hagiasmos* and means "to be set apart for a specific purpose and distinctive use." Hebrews 10:14 uses the word *sanctified* to describe a continuous work in process; that is, we are continually being sanctified.

The work of the Holy Spirit requires certain responses from us—decisions, resolves, and commitments—some reactive and some proactive. Sometimes your response will be confession of sin, sometimes a surrender of a cherished habit that does not please the Lord, and sometimes the laying down of a dream or desire that does not fall in line with God's plan for you. These are reactive, resetting the sails of our lives to catch the wind of the Holy Spirit so we can move in His new direction.

In contrast, proactive ways to set the sail of our lives include listening to God speak through His Word, laying our heart's desires before Him in prayer, and choosing to obey what God says in His Word. Of course, life is complex, with a multitude of decisions, resolves, and commitments all occurring at once. You may be setting your sail before the wind of the Holy Spirit through a simple resolve to quit eating junk food at the same time as a major life decision about whom to marry, what profession to choose, or where to live. The process of setting your sail involves every detail of your life, moment by moment, as you are led by the Holy Spirit.

Finally, surrender may sometimes be so impossibly difficult, you will need to pray, *Lord, I am willing to be made willing.* In this desperate situation, you are submitting yourself completely to God's desire, knowing His ways are best. According to Paul in 1 Corinthians 12:3, no one can say, "Jesus is Lord," except by the Holy Spirit. So if you are willing to be made willing, then God can have His way with you, and oh, how the ship of your life will sail on the ocean of God's love and plan for your life. You will be running before the wind.

Betty Scott Stam's prayer expresses her heart in complete surrender to God: "Lord, I give up all my own plans and purposes, all my own desires and hopes, and accept Thy will for my life. I give myself, my time, my all utterly to Thee to be Thine forever. Fill me and seal me with Thy Holy Spirit. Use me as Thou wilt, send me where Thou wilt, work out Thy whole will in my life at any cost, now and forever." These lofty words seem all too easy for a person to say, but what happens in the midst of adversity? These words might appear trite until you know that Betty Scott Stam and her husband were martyred on the mission field in China for their faith in Christ. This prayer reminds us of Romans 12:1-2, Paul's directive to present our bodies as a living and holy sacrifice through surrender and to renew our minds with the Word of God. Such a prayer requires faith that God's ways are best and His plans are better than our own. God says in Isaiah 55:9, "For as the heavens are higher than the earth, so are My ways higher than your ways and My thoughts than your thoughts."

How do you recognize the wind? How do you know when the Holy Spirit is asking you to set your sail to catch the wind of His powerful move in your life? Henry Blackaby encourages us in his book *Experiencing God* that God is always at work around you. "God speaks by the Holy Spirit through the Bible, prayer, circumstances and the church to reveal Himself, His purposes and His ways." To recognize the move of the Holy Spirit, you must spend quiet time in God's Word and in prayer.

When I am struggling with recognizing the wind of the Holy Spirit, I am helped most by turning to the Bible. God's Word reminds me of the truth about who He is and about His great love, mercy, and desire for a close intimacy with me. These are truths we can hardly believe at times, especially when the heat of a fiery trial has come upon us. But if you look at all the great men and women of God in the Bible, you will immediately see a deep, intimate friendship that God Himself initiates. Did you know that the Lord tarried with Abraham awhile just to be with him and talk with him? In fact, God reasoned within Himself that Abraham was so important to Him that He was compelled to talk with him about the sin in Sodom and Gomorrah (Genesis 18:17-33). The truths about God throughout the Bible will help you give yourself to Him in new ways so that you can run before the wind and set your sail when the winds of His plan change course.

What if there is no wind? What if despite all your best efforts you are unable to recognize the wind of the Holy Spirit? What if you have set your sail and the wind seems to stop? Perhaps the writers of the psalms answer these questions best: "I wait for the LORD, my soul does wait, and in His word do I hope. My soul waits for the Lord more than the watchmen for the morning" (Psalm 130:5-6). When there is seemingly no wind, wait for the Lord, knowing His timing and plan are perfect. Mrs. Charles Cowman, author of *Streams in the Desert,* makes this observation:

> We cannot create the wind or set it in motion, but we can set our sails to catch it when it comes; we cannot make the electricity, but we can stretch the wire along upon which it is to run and do its work; we cannot, in a word, control the Spirit, but we can so place ourselves before the Lord, and so do the things He has bidden us do, that we will come under the influence and power of His mighty breath.[2]

I remember the day, at the age of 17, I stood up with a thousand young men and women and declared, *Here am I, Lord, send me.* That was the day I set my sail so that the Lord could take me on staff with Campus Crusade for Christ. I remember late one night while in seminary, studying the book of Romans, I fell on my face before God and again gave Him every part of myself for His use. That was the day I set my sail so that the wind of God's Spirit could lead me to begin Quiet Time Ministries. I remember the day I met Bob Hawkins Sr., the founder of Harvest House Publishers, who was interested in a book I had written called *Radical Intimacy.* I had no idea at the time what the future would hold. But in laying myself out before the Lord, I set my sail so the Holy Spirit's wind could open the doors to publish *Six Secrets to a Powerful Quiet Time*.

More than once I have surrendered my own desires for ministry to the Lord as He appeared to be closing doors on all my hopes and dreams. By laying these dreams and desires down, I set my sail to catch the wind of the Holy Spirit's move in my life and discovered that His ways were much higher and greater than I had dreamed. When we set our sails to catch His wind, we trade our own small thoughts for His great plan. This does not mean that I have always made the perfect moves in life. In fact, I have made some very stupid mistakes. But the Lord, through His Holy Spirit, has been faithful to convict me where I needed to be convicted, encourage me where I needed His encouragement, and move me forward when I have stumbled. He is the one who has enabled me to set my sail to catch the wind of the Holy Spirit and experience His plans and purposes for me.

My Response

DATE:

KEY VERSE: "Therefore I urge you, brethren, by the mercies of God, to present your bodies a living and holy sacrifice, acceptable to God, which is your spiritual service of worship. And do not be conformed to this world, but be transformed by the renewing of your mind, so that you may prove what the will of God is, that which is good and acceptable and perfect" (Romans 12:1-2).

FOR FURTHER THOUGHT: What does it mean to set your sail to catch the wind of the Holy Spirit moving in your life? What are some ways that you have set your sail in your own life? How has the wind of God's Spirit moved in your own life? Finally, in what ways is God asking you to set your sail today in order to move in His direction? Is there a sin you need to confess, a habit to surrender, an unholy affection to give to Him? Will you give yourself to your Lord? Write a prayer of commitment to the Lord today, expressing all that is on your heart.

MY RESPONSE:

AT THE CROSSROADS

This is what the LORD says: Stop at the crossroads and look around. Ask for the old, godly way, and walk in it. Travel its path, and you will find rest for your souls.

JEREMIAH 6:16 NLT

Your choice to be filled with the Holy Spirit today will determine the course of your life tomorrow. Every day, every moment of your life is consumed with decisions, resolves, and commitments. If you are not going forward in the Christian life, you are effectively going nowhere and, in some cases, going in the wrong direction. Take heed to these words in Jeremiah 6:16 (NLT): "This is what the LORD says: Stop at the crossroads and look around. Ask for the old, godly way, and walk in it. Travel its path, and you will find rest for your souls."

You have seen two snapshots of life: spiritual and fleshly, Spirit-filled and self-propelled, fruit of the Spirit and deeds of the flesh. Will you stop today and look at who you are and where you are going? Which snapshot describes you the best? Are you living for yourself or for the Lord? Which snapshot would you like to resemble the most, Jesus or the world?

Paul encourages us to "examine everything carefully; hold fast to that which is good; abstain from every form of evil" (1 Thessalonians 5:21). The writer of Proverbs tells us that wise people "think about what they do" (Proverbs 14:15 NCV). This is the time to say along with Jeremiah, "But You know me, O LORD; You see me; And You examine my heart's attitude toward You" (Jeremiah 12:3).

God invites a response in Psalm 46:10: "Cease striving and know that I am God." The admonition "cease striving" is a translation of the Hebrew word *raphah* and actually means "Stop! Surrender!" We are about to enter sacred territory on our journey, looking next week at the person and work of the Holy Spirit in greater detail. In preparation for such a journey, stop for a moment to look at yourself and to look at God. Life moves so fast that we often keep going along in a direction without realizing where we are or even what we are doing.

Meditate on Joshua's words to the people of Israel: "Now, therefore, fear the LORD and serve Him in sincerity and truth; and put away the gods which your fathers served beyond the River and in Egypt, and serve the LORD...choose for yourselves today whom you will serve...but as for me and my house, we will serve the LORD" (Joshua 24:14-15). When Joshua said those words, the people responded by saying, "Far be it from us that we should forsake the LORD to serve other gods...We also will serve the LORD, for He is our God" (Joshua 24:16-18). Joshua's challenge moved the people of Israel to express their faith and commitment in tangible ways and with meaningful words, forming a new resolve to follow God.

Now is the time for you to think about who or what has been in control of your life. James McConkey characterizes the Spirit-filled Christian who "ceases to seek all and begins to surrender all" and "no longer seeks the high place, but the lowly one."[1] How can you tell if you have set your sail to catch the wind of the Holy Spirit? Ask yourself the following questions: Do I ask God for direction before I make decisions? Who or what consumes my thoughts most of the time? Do I spend quiet time alone with God? Do I ever tell someone else about Christ? When I sin, and I know I have done wrong, do I confess my sin to God? Am I willing to say no to a good thing when it conflicts with the best thing that God is leading me to do? Am I interested in knowing what God says in His Word, the Bible? Do I talk with God? Do I serve Him in every aspect of my life? Do I love Christ more than myself?

Many in the church are great imitators but not great initiators. I believe many are standing at a crossroads in the church today, watching their sails flap aimlessly, or even worse, huffing and puffing, blowing wind into their own sails. This can only lead to a ship heading in a devastating direction. Some people in the church are so committed to running their own show that the Holy Spirit might not be able to have His way if He did want to move them in a new, incredible direction.

I attended one church conference where the speaker taught about church organization without ever pulling out his Bible as the authority for his belief. He never mentioned Jesus or any principles from the Bible. In the book of Acts, we see the biblical ideal—God initiating the work of ministry through His people. We are told that "The word of God kept on spreading; and the number of disciples continued to increase greatly in Jerusalem" (Acts 6:7), and "the word of the Lord was being spread through the whole region" (Acts 13:49). I believe God is looking for men and women who will turn to Him, trust Him, listen to what He says in the Bible, and lay their requests before Him in prayer. I believe God is looking for those men and women who want to see Him do something in and through them that only He can do through the power of the Holy Spirit.

Perhaps you are standing at a crossroads in your life. Maybe things have not turned out the way you thought they would. Maybe you have even given up on God. Now is the time for you to say, *Lord, I'm sorry. Fill me anew with your Holy Spirit and fulfill in me what You have planned.*

Maybe you have been faithfully serving the Lord out of love for Him, but no one has come alongside to cheer you onward. Dear friend, you can know that even if everyone deserts you, the Lord stands with you. Today is the day for you to say once again, *Lord, I love you. Fill me with your Holy Spirit and continue to empower me for those things You have called me to accomplish.* Heaven is going to tell the story of all that God has done in and through those who belong to Him. Heaven will reveal what happened when we were willing to lay aside our small dreams and lay hold of the big dreams of God. Heaven will declare the greatness of living life in the power of the Holy Spirit.

What if Billy Graham had never run to God for guidance when he was wrestling over the authority of God's Word? He was losing such confidence to preach early in his life that he went to Henrietta Mears and J. Edwin Orr, his contemporaries at a Forest Home conference, and told them he felt he should just sit in the audience. Wisely, they prayed with Billy Graham and urged him to preach. Their decision to keep him on their ministry team forced Billy Graham to deal with his doubts and spiritual struggle. Billy Graham ran to God and was brought to a place of decision and resolve about the Bible. As a result, he preached with the power and confidence that led to a lifetime of evangelistic crusades.

What if D.L. Moody had not said yes to God in the back room of a store where he worked as a shoe salesman? What if G. Campbell Morgan, in the midst of his doubts about the Bible's authority, had not locked all his other books in a cupboard and sat down with the Word of God to find out what God had to say? And what if in the midst of living for myself in college, I had never thought through the words of Jesus, "I am the way, and the truth, and the life," and decided to follow the truth rather than myself?

The decisions, resolves, and commitments at the crossroads alter the course of our lives. We are brought to these choices by the work of the Holy Spirit. "God is working in you, giving you the desire and the power to do what pleases him" (Philippians 2:13 NLT). You can count on God to continue working in you all the days of your life until you are face-to-face with Him, stepping from time into eternity. Paul says, "I am certain that God, who began the good work within you, will continue his work until it is finally finished on the day when Christ Jesus returns" (Philippians 1:6). Time is short, and eternity is forever. May you continually, day by day, choose to set your sail to catch the wind of the Holy Spirit and walk in His power.

As you close your time with the Lord today, meditate on these words by Annie Johnson Flint:

The Set of the Sail
I stood on the shore beside the sea;
The wind from the West blew fresh and free,
While past the rocks at the harbor's mouth

The ships went North, and the ships went South,
And some sailed out on an unknown quest,
And some sailed into the harbor's rest;
Yet ever the wind blew out from the West.

I said to one who had sailed the sea
That this was a marvel unto me;
For how can the ships go safely forth,
Some to the South and some to the North,
Far out to sea on the golden quest,
Or in to the harbor's calm and rest,
And ever the wind blew out of the West?

The sailor smiled as he answered me,
"Go where you will when you're on the sea,
Though head winds baffle and flaws delay,
You can keep the course by night and day,
Drive with the breeze or against the gale;
It will not matter what winds prevail,
For all depends on the set of the sail."

Voyager soul on the sea of life,
O'er waves of sorrow and sin and strife,
When fogs bewilder and foes betray,
Steer straight on your course from day to day;
Though unseen currents run deep and swift,
Where rocks are hidden and sandbars shift,
All helpless and aimless, you need not drift.

Oh, set your sail to the heavenly gale,
And then, no matter what winds prevail,
No reef shall wreck you, no calm delay,
No mist shall hinder, no storm shall stay;
Though far you wander and long you roam,
Though salt sea-spray and o'er white sea-foam,
No wind that can blow but shall speed you home.[2]

ANNIE JOHNSON FLINT

My Response

DATE:

KEY VERSE: "This is what the LORD says: Stop at the crossroads and look around. Ask for the old, godly way, and walk in it. Travel its path, and you will find rest for your souls" (Jeremiah 6:16 NLT).

FOR FURTHER THOUGHT: Where are you today with the Lord? Are you yielding to Him and walking in the power of the Holy Spirit? What is the most important truth you learned from your reading today?

MY RESPONSE:

Day Six

QUIET TIME
WEEK ONE:
A HEART ON FIRE
FOR CHRIST

*And they said to one another, Were not
our hearts greatly moved and burning
within us while He was talking with us on
the road and as He opened and explained
to us [the sense of] the Scriptures?*

LUKE 24:32 AMP

PREPARE YOUR HEART

This week you have seen the kind of life God has made possible for
you through the Holy Spirit. You have discovered that the Spirit-filled
life is the normal Christian life intended for every believer in Christ.
Men and women through the centuries who loved God and whose hearts
burned for Christ drew on the power of the Holy Spirit.

F.B. Meyer was a radical Christian in his day. He was kind and gentle
but not weak—he demonstrated power under control. He grew up in a
Christian home and learned early on about the spiritual things that matter most. Meyer felt called to be a preacher, graduated from Regent's Park
College, and served as a pastor at Priory Street Baptist Chapel.

In 1871 D.L. Moody and Ira Sankey ministered at Meyer's church. One night Moody preached on the Holy Spirit. Meyer was so convicted, he wrestled two days with God. He surrendered to God and ministered in a new way, filled with the power of the Holy Spirit. Moody taught him to be himself and allow the Holy Spirit to do a mighty work in and through him. Moody's sermons lit a fire in Meyer's soul, and Meyer caught a glimpse of a wider, larger life in which there "was but one standard by which to measure men, namely their devotion to, and knowledge of, the Son of God."[1]

Meyer pastored a number of churches in England and ministered often in the United States. Spurgeon said that "Meyer preaches as a man who has seen God face to face." J. Wilbur Chapman's ministry was transformed after he read a printed sermon by F.B. Meyer. Chapman said, "I owe more to this man than to anyone in the world." Meyer wrote more than 30 books, some expository and others devotional, but all challenging to a life of devotion to God. He always claimed that he was an ordinary man and that the Lord could do the same through anyone who was yielded to Him.[2] The ripple effect of a life is caused by a heart on fire for Christ.

Turn to God now and ask Him to quiet your heart and speak to you in His Word about having a heart on fire for Him.

READ AND STUDY GOD'S WORD

1. Today you are going to briefly look at what it means to have a heart on fire. Read Luke 24:13-35 and write out all that you learn about why and when the hearts of the two men on the road to Emmaus began to burn for the Lord.

2. A heart on fire is committed to Jesus Christ. Look at the following verses and record everything you learn about what it means to be committed to the Lord:

Romans 12:1-2

Philippians 3:7-14

Hebrews 12:1-3

3. Summarize your most significant insights about what it means to live for Christ and follow Him.

4. When your heart is on fire for Christ, how can your life make a difference in the lives of those around you?

ADORE GOD IN PRAYER

Draw near to the Lord and pray, *Lord, set my heart on fire.*

YIELD YOURSELF TO GOD

Meditate on these words by F.B. Meyer:

> We are called on to present our bodies as instruments of righteousness, because all true regimen of the inner life immediately affects the body in all its members; and conversely, the consecration of the body reacts upon and affects the temper of the soul. It would be well for you to take Miss Havergal's hymn ["Take My Life and Let It Be"], with its enumeration of the various parts of the body, and offer and present yourself, to be from this day and forward, wholly for God. Only believe that He is more anxious for this than words can tell, because He loves you so, and that He accepts immediately what you offer.
>
> Such consecration must be living; that is, it must enter into all our life, being holy, well-pleasing to God, and rational. It is not only reasonable when we consider the relation we sustain to Him, but it should engage all our intelligence and reasoning faculties. And when it is made, and the soul is becoming duly transfigured in its exercise, we begin to prove that God's will, which once we dreaded, is also good, well-pleasing, and perfect. When we look at God's will from a distance, and before consecration, it seems impossible. It is only when we begin to obey, that we can say: *Thou sweet beloved will of God.*[3]

ENJOY HIS PRESENCE

Have you given yourself to your Lord? Take some time now and pray through the words of the hymn "Take My Life and Let It Be" by Francis Havergal:

> Take my life and let it be consecrated, Lord, to Thee;
> Take my moments and my days—let them flow in ceaseless praise,
> Let them flow in ceaseless praise.

Take my hands and let them move at the impulse of Thy love;
Take my feet and let them be swift and beautiful for Thee,
Swift and beautiful for Thee.

Take my voice and let me sing always, only, for my King;
Take my lips and let them be filled with messages from Thee,
Filled with messages from Thee.

Take my silver and my gold—not a mite would I withhold;
Take my intellect and use every power as Thou shalt choose,
Every power as Thou shalt choose.

Take my will and make it Thine—it shall be no longer mine;
Take my heart—it is Thine own, it shall be Thy royal throne,
It shall be Thy royal throne.

Take my love—my Lord, I pour at Thy feet its treasure store;
Take myself—and I will be ever, only, all for Thee,
Ever, only, all for Thee.

REST IN HIS LOVE

With eyes wide open to the mercies of God, I beg you, my
brothers, as an act of intelligent worship, to give him your
bodies, as a living sacrifice, consecrated to him and acceptable
by him. Don't let the world around you squeeze you into its
own mould, but let God re-mould your minds from within,
so that you may prove in practice that the plan of God for
you is good, meets all his demands and moves towards the
goal of true maturity (Romans 12:1-2 PHILLIPS).

Notes — Week One

Week Two

THE PERSON OF
THE HOLY SPIRIT

Days 7–12

HE IS YOUR GOD

*In the beginning God created the heavens
and the earth. The earth was formless and
void, and darkness was over the surface of
the deep, and the Spirit of God was moving
over the surface of the waters...Then God
said, Let Us make man in Our image.*

GENESIS 1:1-2,26

⤵

The Holy Spirit is the third person of the triune God, not merely an abstract idea, an ingenious influence, or a whimsical wish. The Holy Spirit is not separate in any way from God the Father or God the Son. God is one, yet triune—three in one. When God said, "Let Us make man in Our image" (Genesis 1:26), He revealed both His oneness and His plurality. Throughout the Bible, we learn more about the Trinity: God is the Father, the Son (Jesus Christ), and the Holy Spirit.

The Holy Spirit was present in the beginning. We learn in Genesis 1:2 that the "Spirit of God was moving over the surface of the waters." The triune God, the Trinity, is an incomprehensible mystery (Deuteronomy 29:29, Romans 11:33-36), yet His person, His nature, and His existence are true and real and do not in any way depend on our own comprehension or understanding of Him. He is who He is, and His person is the objective reality, the ultimate measure of all that is true and real.[1] Because He is incomprehensible, we cannot know everything about Him, but we can know Him as He reveals Himself to us. This secret of knowing God is critical to our faith.

How can we know that the Holy Spirit is God? The Word of God reveals His divine person, His attributes and personality.

- He was involved with the Father and Son in creation, "moving over the surface of the waters" (Genesis 1:2).

- He brought about the incarnation of Christ: "[The child who] has been conceived in her is of the Holy Spirit" (Matthew 1:20).

- He gives life: "The law of the Spirit of life in Christ Jesus has set you free from the law of sin and death" (Romans 8:2).

- He is omniscient (all-knowing): "The Spirit searches all things, even the depths of God. For who among men knows the thoughts of a man except the spirit of the man which is in him? Even so the thoughts of God no one knows except the Spirit of God" (1 Corinthians 2:10-11).

- He is omnipotent (all-powerful): "The Spirit of God has made me, and the breath of the Almighty gives me life" (Job 33:4).

- He is omnipresent (present everywhere at the same time): "Where can I go from Your Spirit? Or where can I flee from Your presence?" (Psalm 139:7).

- He is eternal: "How much more will the blood of Christ, who through the eternal Spirit offered Himself without blemish to God?" (Hebrews 9:14).

- He transforms human hearts: "You are a letter of Christ, cared for by us, written not with ink but with the Spirit of the living God, not on tablets of stone but on tablets of human hearts" (2 Corinthians 3:3).

- He is the Spirit of truth: "He [will] be with you forever; that is, the Spirit of truth, whom the world cannot receive" (John 14:16-17).

- He inspired the Word of God: "But know this first of all, that no prophecy of Scripture is a matter of one's own interpretation, for no prophecy was ever made by an act of human will, but men moved by the Holy Spirit spoke from God" (2 Peter 1:21).

How can we know that the Holy Spirit is a person with personality? He thinks with intellect and purposes with will and feels with emotion. The apostles implied the presence of the Holy Spirit's intellect and reasoning when they wrote, "It seemed good to the Holy Spirit and to us" (Acts 15:28). In the entire book of Acts, the Holy Spirit works in and through the church with a purposeful will. In Acts 13:2,4, the Holy Spirit spoke to those in the church at Antioch: "The Holy Spirit said, 'Set apart for Me Barnabas and Saul for the work to which I called them...' So, being sent out by the Holy Spirit, they went down to Seleucia and from there they sailed to Cyprus." He loves, for in Romans 15:30 we read of the "love of the Spirit." In addition, we learn that the Holy Spirit can be grieved, for Paul exhorts those at Ephesus, "Do not grieve the Holy Spirit of God" (Ephesians 4:30).

How can we understand the many facets of the Holy Spirit? The Bible offers a number of metaphors for the person and work of the Holy Spirit:

Wind. Jesus, in talking about the Holy Spirit, said, "The wind blows where it wishes and you hear the sound of it, but do not know where it comes from and where it is going; so is everyone who is born of the Spirit" (John 3:8). On the Day of Pentecost, the coming of the Holy Spirit is described as a "violent rushing wind" (Acts 2:2). The Greek word translated "Spirit" is *pneuma,* which means "breath." The Holy Spirit is literally the breath of God. This is the origin of pneumatology, the study of the Holy Spirit, a vital doctrine in systematic theology classes. In this metaphor of wind, we see not only the sovereignty of God but also the mighty unseen power of God as the Holy Spirit accomplishes highly visible results in believers' lives.

Fire. In Isaiah 4:4, the Holy Spirit is called the spirit of burning. In Matthew 3:11, John the Baptist said that Jesus would baptize with the Holy Spirit and fire. Then, in Acts 2:3 on the Day of Pentecost, the Holy Spirit came in the visible form of fire resting on each disciple. J. Oswald Sanders, in his book *The Holy Spirit of Promise,* says, "Just as the fiery sun is the source of power in the solar realm, so the Holy Spirit is the source of omnipotent power in the moral and spiritual realm. The fire of the Spirit produces boldness and zeal in those on whom it falls."[2]

Water. In John 7:38-39 Jesus declares, " 'He who believes in Me, as the Scripture said, "From his innermost being will flow rivers of living water."' But this He spoke of the Spirit." In this metaphor of rivers of living water, we learn that the Holy Spirit is our unceasing source of life and power.

Dove. While Jesus was praying following His baptism, the Bible says that "heaven was opened, and the Holy Spirit descended upon Him in bodily form like a dove" (Luke 3:21-22). The dove is a fitting symbol of the Holy Spirit as it is fond of home, a bird of peace and love, and according to Isaiah 38:14 will actually mourn when deprived of fellowship. This metaphor of the dove emphasizes the peaceful, loving, relational, and nurturing qualities of God.

Seal. The Holy Spirit is likened to a seal of authenticity three times in the New Testament (2 Corinthians 1:22; Ephesians 1:13-14; 4:30). He is our proof of salvation, our guarantee of divine ownership, and our assurance of acceptance.

Oil. The Holy Spirit is associated with anointing oil in various places throughout Scripture, such as Luke 4:18; Acts 4:27; 10:38; 2 Corinthians 1:21; 1 John 2:20,27. Our anointing by the Holy Spirit sets us apart as priests and kings, for Jesus has "made us to be a kingdom, priests to His God and Father" (Revelation 1:6).

The Holy Spirit is God, a multifaceted person with personality. So what should be our response to the Holy Spirit, and what does it mean for us to know that He is God? That these truths require an attitude of awe and reverence is an understatement. We should not treat the Holy Spirit as a casual dinner guest or an indifferent bystander in our lives. We should not ignore Him. We certainly cannot cast Him aside as we would an idea or a vaguely holy influence.

Samuel Chadwick, a noted English preacher of the late 1800s, recalls discovering the vital importance of the Holy Spirit in his ministry. As a lay preacher he had been taught to prepare sermons with meticulous care. He mistakenly believed that if a minister preached interesting sermons, people would automatically flock to his church to listen to him. As he says, "Soon my little stock of excellent sermons was exhausted, and nothing much had happened."

Almost in desperation, he persuaded his friends to enter into a covenant with him to pray for revival by the Holy Spirit. His crisis of obedience ultimately led to a dark night of the soul. "Soon the Holy Spirit was searching and convicting me," the struggle persisting into the early hours of a Sunday morning. Finally, he rose from his knees, took his precious stock of old sermon manuscripts, threw them into the empty grate, and set fire to them. As he exclaims, "Things began to happen."

The very next day his preaching led to seven conversions, more than in the previous seven years of ministry. During the weeks that followed, hundreds were converted. He says, "Some of the most wicked people in the neighborhood were converted and changed into saints." In Samuel Chadwick's case, surrendering to the Holy Spirit was his key to the Scriptures—his thinking, his service, and his life. The Holy Spirit is the third person of the Trinity, so like Chadwick, we must pay attention to His person and work in our lives and regard Him with awe and reverence. "O fear the Lord, you His saints; for to those who fear Him there is no want" (Psalm 34:9).

My Response

DATE:

KEY VERSE: "In the beginning God created the heavens and the earth. The earth was formless and void, and darkness was over the surface of the deep, and the Spirit of God was moving over the surface of the waters" (Genesis 1:1-2).

FOR FURTHER THOUGHT: What is the most important truth you learned today about the Holy Spirit? How have you seen Him at work in your life?

MY RESPONSE:

Day Eight

HE IS YOUR SALVATION

Jesus answered, "Truly, truly, I say to you,
unless one is born of water and the Spirit
he cannot enter into the kingdom of God."

JOHN 3:5

≫

The Holy Spirit is the author of your new birth in Christ. All that happens in your life to bring you to salvation comes to you through the Holy Spirit. Addressing this very point, a ruler of the Jews, a Pharisee named Nicodemus, came to Jesus hidden in the shadows of the night to question Him about His true identity. Jesus saw into Nicodemus' searching soul and responded to his deepest need for salvation. He said, "Truly, truly, I say to you, unless one is born again he cannot see the kingdom of God unless one is born of water and the Spirit he cannot enter the kingdom of God" (John 3:3,5).

Perhaps the most exceptional display of the Spirit's work in a conversion is described in detail in the book of Acts. Saul of Tarsus had begun his career of persecuting Christians. We are first made aware of Saul's premeditation and complicity in Christian persecution at the stoning of Stephen in Acts 7:54-60. Recall that those who stoned Stephen for his faith in Christ laid their robes at the feet of the "young man named Saul." But the Holy Spirit was already at work in Saul's heart, constraining him to hear the powerful witness of Stephen just before his gruesome death. Stephen called out, "Lord Jesus, receive my spirit," collapsed to his knees, and cried out with a loud voice, "Lord, do not hold this sin against them!" (Acts 7:59-60). In the next few verses, we see that "Saul was in hearty agreement with putting him to death," for all appearances a hardened heart leading the beginning of a great persecution against the church in Jerusalem. Luke leaves no doubt that Saul was a significant player in that persecution; Saul "began ravaging the church, entering house after house, and dragging off men and women, he would put them in prison" (Acts 8:3).

As so often happens, a fervent witness for Christ does not fall on deaf ears. One can only imagine what was on Saul's mind as he was traveling on the road to Damascus in hot pursuit of Christians scattered by the persecution. Acts 9:1 says Saul was "breathing threats and murder against the disciples." But perhaps Saul had more on his mind than his evil tasks. Perhaps he was even grappling with Stephen's compelling words.

Suddenly a light from heaven flashed around him. Saul, a Pharisee with letters of condemnation for Christians in his hand from the high priest at Jerusalem, fell to the ground, hearing the voice of Jesus speaking directly to Him. "Saul, Saul, why are you persecuting Me?" The only words that surfaced for Saul were, "Who are You, Lord?" And Jesus said, "I am Jesus whom you are persecuting, but get up and enter into the city and it will be told you what you must do" (Acts 9:4-6).

Sometime during Saul's dramatic encounter with Jesus, he was blinded and required help to be led to a home in Damascus. For the next three long days, Saul certainly had time to think about what had happened to him. And sometime during those three days, Saul's spiritual eyes were opened, for we discover in Acts 9:11 that Saul was praying. At this same time, the Lord instructed a man named Ananias to go to Saul in Damascus and lay his hands on him that he might regain his sight. Ananias was apprehensive about this command from the Lord because the news of Saul's hatred for Christians had spread like wildfire. The Lord said to him, "Go, for he is a chosen instrument of Mine, to bear my name before the Gentiles and kings and the sons of Israel" (verse 15).

Ananias went to Saul, laid his hands on him, and said, "Brother Saul, the Lord Jesus, who appeared to you on the road by which you were coming, has sent me so that you may regain your sight and be filled with the Holy Spirit." Immediately Saul regained his sight and began to "proclaim Jesus in the synagogues, saying 'He is the Son of God'" (verse 20). This Saul, the Christian persecutor, became Paul the apostle, one of the greatest Christian believers this world has ever known and writer of many books in our New Testament canon.

Nothing is as exciting as hearing about someone's conversion to Christ. I will never forget the day I shared the gospel with a young woman at the zoo in Honolulu. I had seen her sitting on a bench alone. It was late in the day, and I was tired, so I sat down beside her and began talking with her. I soon discovered she was a Mormon, so I began sharing how Jesus had died on the cross for our sins. Before long, I saw a new understanding in her eyes, and so I asked if she wanted to pray and receive Jesus into her heart and life. She said, "Oh yes, I would!" And so, together, we sat and prayed to the Lord, and that dear woman asked Jesus Christ to come into her life, forgive her sins, and give her eternal life.

When we were finished praying, she looked at me with eyes just shining and said, "It is as though once I was blind, but now I see."

I said to her, "You know, there's a hymn with those very words." And sitting there on that bench, I sang to her, "Amazing grace, how sweet the sound, that saved a wretch like me. I once was lost, but now am found. Was blind, but now I see." We shared tears of joy. Oh, what a day when the old becomes new and the spiritually blind can now see.

Again and again, the Holy Spirit does His work to save one person after another. The logical question is this: What then is the role of the Holy Spirit in salvation?

Conviction. The Holy Spirit convicts the world of sin, righteousness and judgment according to Jesus in John 16:8-11. He reveals to the unbeliever that he is a sinner in need of a Savior. He enlightens the unbeliever to see his need for the righteousness of God through believing in Christ. He also reveals to the unbeliever that God judged sin when Jesus was on the cross opening the way to God.

Regeneration. When a person believes in Christ, he or she is then born again by the Spirit (John 3:5-6). The born-again believer is a new person. "Therefore if anyone is in Christ, he is a new creature; the old things passed away; behold, new things have come" (2 Corinthians 5:17). Spiritual blindness becomes spiritual sight as the veil lying over a heart is removed. "Whenever a person turns to the Lord, the veil is taken away" (2 Corinthians 3:16).

Indwelling. The Holy Spirit makes His home in the believer forever. Paul says, "However, you are not in the flesh, but in the Spirit, if indeed the Spirit of God dwells in you. But if anyone does not have the Spirit of Christ, he does not belong to Him" (Romans 8:9). This indwelling is a great assurance to believers—all Christians have the Holy Spirit. This indwelling can never be lost (1 John 5:11-12).

Baptism. The Holy Spirit unites you with Christ forever and places you into the body of Christ. "By one Spirit we were all baptized into one body, whether Jews or Greeks, whether slaves or free, and we were all made to drink of one Spirit" (1 Corinthians 12:13). All Christians are baptized by the Holy Spirit, uniting them with Christ. What some have called another baptism following salvation is actually the filling of the Holy Spirit. Your union with Christ includes righteousness, sanctification, and redemption (1 Corinthians 1:30).

Sealing. The Holy Spirit is your mark of ownership, signifying you belong to God and will live forever with Him. "Now He who establishes us with you in Christ and anointed us is God, who also sealed us and gave us the Spirit in our hearts as a pledge" (2 Corinthians 1:21-22).

Filling. The Holy Spirit fills you, controlling and empowering you again and again as you walk with the Lord through life. "Don't be drunk with wine, because that will ruin your life. Instead, be filled with the Holy Spirit" (Ephesians 5:18 NLT).

Assurance. The Holy Spirit is one of the assurances of your salvation, along with the trustworthiness of God's promises in John 1:11-12; Romans 10:9; and 1 John 5:14-15. Paul says, "The Spirit Himself testifies with our spirit that we are children of God" (Romans 8:16).

Charles Finney was born in 1792 and grew up in New York. At the age of 29, he became an attorney, thoroughly intent on practicing the law. Finney believed the Bible to be the Word of God, but he admitted he knew nothing about the gospel of Christ. His reading of the Bible eventually led him to become concerned for his own salvation. He began thinking about the righteousness of God and saw the finished work of Christ and His atonement for sins in a new light. He realized his need to receive Christ. Following the prompting of the Holy Spirit through his reading of the Word of God, he cried out to the Lord, "Lord, I take Thee at Thy word."[1]

Charles Finney became a preacher and five years later began conducting revival meetings. He became one of the inspirational leaders of the Second Great Awakening in America in the 1800s and is often referred to as America's foremost revivalist by church historians. Charles Finney, a lawyer converted into a preacher; D.L. Moody, a shoe salesman transformed into an evangelist; John Newton, a slave trader regenerated into a hymn writer and minister…the great story is told again and again—"the old things passed away; behold new things have come" (2 Corinthians 5:17). How does such a miraculous change occur in people's hearts? One way only—through the salvation work of the Holy Spirit.

Always remember, dear friend, the Holy Spirit accomplishes His saving work with perfection. Regardless of how lost someone in your life may seem, there is hope because of what God has promised to accomplish. What is your own response? First, if you do not know Christ and have never invited Him into your life, you need to make that decision immediately. Simply pray and ask Him to come into your life: *Lord Jesus, I need You. Thank You for dying on the cross for my sins. I ask You now to come into my life, forgive my sins, and make me the person You want me to become, in Jesus' name. Amen.*

If you do know Jesus as your Lord and Savior, thank Him for the excellent work of the Holy Spirit in giving you everlasting life and causing you to be born again. If you have friends or family who do not know the Lord, keep on telling them about Jesus with your life and your words. Pray for them. You can know that God is at work, and when you least expect it, a person can turn his or her life over to Him. Believe God for this promise and trust Him to do something amazing and wonderful, "far more abundantly beyond all that we ask or think" (Ephesians 3:20).

My Response

DATE:

KEY VERSE: Jesus answered, "Truly, truly, I say to you, unless one is born of water and the Spirit he cannot enter into the kingdom of God" (John 3:5).

FOR FURTHER THOUGHT: Describe what the Holy Spirit does to bring about your salvation. What did you learn from the examples of the apostle Paul and Charles Finney? Write a prayer to the Lord, thanking Him for what He has done in your own life.

MY RESPONSE:

Day Nine

HE IS YOUR
COMFORTER

*And I will ask the Father, and He will
give you another Comforter (Counselor,
Helper, Intercessor, Advocate, Strengthener,
and Standby), that He may remain with
you forever—the Spirit of Truth.*

JOHN 14:16-17 AMP

⋙

The Holy Spirit dwells in your life through the prayer of Jesus Himself. When Jesus prays to the Father on our behalf, His words must command our attention, for the Father knows our need even when we do not understand or know it for ourselves (Matthew 6:8). Following Jesus' revelation to His disciples that He was going away, Jesus prayed to His Father on our behalf (John 14:3,16-17). I like the Amplified version here as it opens up the Scripture, painting a picture with the words "Comforter," "receive," and "lives with you." "And I will ask the Father, and He will give you another Comforter (Counselor, Helper, Intercessor, Advocate, Strengthener, and Standby), that He may remain with you forever—the Spirit of Truth, Whom the world cannot receive (welcome, take to its heart), because it does not see Him or know and recognize Him. But you know and recognize Him, for He lives with you [constantly] and will be in you" (John 14:16-17 AMP).

Jesus revealed what He wants for us—"another Comforter." The word "another" is a translation of the Greek word *allon,* which means "one of the same kind." Jesus was saying He was going to send a Comforter to His disciples, a Helper like Himself. The Greek word translated "Comforter" is *parakletos* and describes someone who is called to the side of for the purpose of helping.[1] Commentators often refer to the Holy Spirit as the Paraclete because of the Greek word used here for the Holy Spirit. The word implies that the Holy Spirit will give Jesus' disciples everything they need for every circumstance of life. The Helper, the Holy Spirit, will help you, doing for you what you cannot do for yourself.

Have you ever been stuck in the middle of the road because your car has broken down? You could do nothing to fix your car. But then the tow truck pulled up alongside, hooked your car to it, and drove it to the repair shop. F.B. Meyer describes the Paraclete as "One who would adjust Himself to their needs with that quickness of perception, and sufficiency of resource, which characterize a personal Leader and Administrator…a strong, wise, ever-present Personality…to abide with you forever."[2]

God has a great desire to help you. We see His desire more clearly when He says, "Do not fear, for I am with you; do not anxiously look about you, for I am your God. I will strengthen you, surely I will help you, surely I will uphold you with My righteous right hand" (Isaiah 41:10). The Hebrew word translated "help" is *azar.* It's used 80 times in the Old Testament and means to support and to give material or non-material encouragement. David surely knew the ever-present help of the Lord when he said, "In the day of my trouble I shall call upon You, for You will answer me. There is no one like You among the gods, O LORD, nor are there any works like Yours" (Psalm 86:7-8). Charles Spurgeon places the manifold help of our Paraclete in holy perspective in his classic devotional *Morning and Evening:*

> O my soul, is not this enough? Dost thou need more strength than the omnipotence of the United Trinity? Dost thou want more wisdom than exists in the Father, more love than displays itself in the Son, or more power than is

manifest in the influences of the Spirit? Bring hither thine empty pitcher! Surely this well will fill it. Haste, gather up thy wants and bring them here—thine emptiness, thy woes, thy needs. Behold, this river of God is full for thy supply... The Eternal God is thine helper![3]

Why, then, did Jesus want you to know, experience, and be indwelt by the Holy Spirit? Jesus answers this question with an enigmatic statement given to His disciples at perhaps their most vulnerable time—just prior to His betrayal and capture. He said, "I tell you the truth, it is to your advantage that I go away; for if I do not go away, the Helper will not come to you; but if I go, I will send Him to you" (John 16:7). How can this be? The disciples had known the deepest intimacy of the very presence of the God of the universe Himself. If Jesus' presence was withdrawn, this must be a great loss. How could Jesus' departure be better for the disciples? Jesus' words in John 14–16—His Farewell Discourse, spoken to His disciples just prior to His arrest—supply many reasons the coming of the Holy Spirit is good news for all believers:

The Holy Spirit will be with you forever. Jesus explains, "He will give you another Helper, that He may be with you forever" (John 14:16). Do you catch the finality in this declaration? The Holy Spirit will never be withdrawn; He will never leave voluntarily or be taken away by outside forces but instead dwells within you forever. This is one of the most beautiful and personal truths for believers. Your God is not distant and far away, not with you one day and gone the next. Have you experienced peace in the midst of a storm? That's the Holy Spirit at work in your life.

The Holy Spirit constantly provides the resources you need to live life. You have someone in your life who knows your needs better than you do, one who supplies you with resources when, where, and how you need them. The early church is our great example: "So the church throughout all Judea and Galilee and Samaria enjoyed peace, being built up; and going on in the fear of the Lord and in the comfort of the Holy Spirit, it continued to increase" (Acts 9:31). Have you ever had a need that was met from an unexpected resource? That's the Holy Spirit at work in your life.

The Holy Spirit enables you to personally experience the Lord's presence. Jesus said, "In that day you will know that I am in My Father, and you in Me, and I in you" (John 14:20). He continues by saying, "We will come to him and make Our abode with him" (John 14:23). Oh, what a powerful promise! The Lord is no longer with you as He had been with the disciples, but rather living in you because of the indwelling Holy Spirit. Have you ever sensed the reality of the presence of the Lord Jesus with you? That's the Holy Spirit at work in your life.

The Holy Spirit allows Jesus to continue His ministry on earth in and through you. Jesus affirms, "Truly, truly, I say to you, he who believes in Me, the works that I do, he will do also; and greater works than these he will do, because I go to the Father" (John 14:12). Have you ever done something in ministry far beyond your human limitations? Perhaps speaking in front of an audience, leading a Bible study, or organizing a church event? That's the Holy Spirit at work in your life.

The Holy Spirit comforts you and will never leave you all alone. Jesus entreats us, "I will not leave you as orphans; I will come to you" (John 14:18). He promises His presence as your Comforter. Have you ever experienced comfort in a desperate situation? That's the Holy Spirit at work in your life.

The Holy Spirit glorifies Christ. Jesus said, "He will glorify Me, for He will take of Mine and will disclose it to you" (John 16:14). The Holy Spirit always turns the soul's gaze to Christ and never draws attention to Himself. This, in fact, is the great test of a church's orthodoxy—are you drawn to Christ? Have you ever seen the character of Christ expressed in your life in a new way? That's the Holy Spirit at work in your life.

The Holy Spirit teaches you objective truth. Jesus said, "He will teach you all things" (John 14:26). "But when He, the Spirit of truth, comes, He will guide you into all truth" (John 16:13). Have you ever been confused about a church doctrine, a leader's beliefs, or even a single biblical passage, and then suddenly you were able to see the truth? That's the Holy Spirit at work in your life.

The Holy Spirit helps you remember the Word of God. Jesus said the Holy Spirit "will bring to your remembrance all that I said to you" (John 14:26). The Holy Spirit reminds you of God's Word, making it the source of your attitudes and beliefs. Has a verse from the Bible ever come into your mind at precisely at the right time? That's the Holy Spirit at work in your life.

In *They Found the Secret,* V. Raymond Edman shared the stories of 20 men and women who lived powerful lives for Jesus Christ, such as J. Hudson Taylor, Andrew Murray, and Oswald Chambers. What was their secret? They drew on the power of the Holy Spirit and experienced the indwelling life of Jesus Christ in their own lives.

Fast forward to the bedside of Dr. Bill Bright, founder of Campus Crusade for Christ, several weeks before his death from pulmonary fibrosis. Vonette Bright says she asked her husband about his suffering, and she recounts his reply: "With the brightest eyes, he said, 'I am not suffering. Jesus suffered.'"

Here was a man who relied upon the Comforter for wisdom in the midst of his final trial. Bill Bright completed his book *The Journey Home* with the Comforter's help only three weeks before his death. The Comforter had led him to found Campus Crusade for Christ from the humble beginnings of a $200 a month rented house near the campus of UCLA. The Comforter infused him with the idea for *The Four Spiritual Laws,* an evangelistic tract that has led countless souls to salvation on campuses all over the world. The Comforter enabled him to stand for Christ in front of the political heat of a Florida Legislature as he offered the opening prayer.

Dr. Bill Bright knew the Comforter's help throughout his entire life, even to the end. Bill Bright's son, Bradley, recalls his father's Spirit-filled devotional life in the midst of suffering. "For the next hour I saw him try and read his Bible. He would wake up and fall asleep. He was trying to spend time with his Lord, even with the haze of medication. That was a phenomenal example to me of what made a man successful."

You see, dear friend, the great men and women of Christ knew the secret of the Spirit-filled life. May that be your secret as well! Draw upon the life-giving power of God as you keep in step with His great gift, the Comforter, who gives you everything you need for every circumstance of life.

My Response

DATE:

KEY VERSE: "And I will ask the Father, and He will give you another Comforter (Counselor, Helper, Intercessor, Advocate, Strengthener, and Standby), that He may remain with you forever—the Spirit of Truth, Whom the world cannot receive (welcome, take to its heart), because it does not see Him or know and recognize Him. But you know and recognize Him, for He lives with you [constantly] and will be in you" (John 14:16-17 AMP).

FOR FURTHER THOUGHT: What is your favorite truth about the Holy Spirit from your reading today? Jesus calls the Holy Spirit another Comforter, or Paraclete. What does that name mean? Think about all the reasons Jesus wanted you to have the Holy Spirit. Will you write a prayer to Him, thanking Him for asking the Father to give you the Holy Spirit?

MY RESPONSE:

Day Ten

HE IS YOUR
INDWELLING GLORY

*Do you not know that you are
a temple of God and that the
Spirit of God dwells in you?*

1 Corinthians 3:16

T he Lord lives in you through the power and presence of the indwelling Holy Spirit. Paul exhorted the church at Corinth, "Do you not know that you are a temple of God and that the Spirit of God dwells in you?" (1 Corinthians 3:16). Once you have been born again spiritually, your body literally houses the Spirit of God Himself. It is a sacred temple, a sanctuary. Such an amazing act of God does not come about by chance but by His own purposeful intent and desire. God loves you and desires to live with you, know you, and fellowship with you forever. That is why John said, "Indeed our fellowship is with the Father, and with His Son Jesus Christ" (1 John 1:3). How does He live in you? Through the indwelling Holy Spirit.

Paul's reference to the church as a temple of God makes more sense if we look at the Old Testament tabernacle. At the outset of Israel's wilderness journey, God instructed Moses to build a tabernacle, also called "a tent of meeting." The tabernacle was the place where God lived with His people, met with them, spoke with them, and set them apart by filling it with His glory (Exodus 25:8; 29:43-50; 40:34-38). Paul makes clear that the Old Testament tabernacle is a "picture" of the New Testament indwelling of the Holy Spirit.

Just as the tabernacle had only one entrance, Jesus Christ is our only entrance to God's presence (John 10:9; 14:6). Just as the altar of brass held sin offerings, so Jesus Christ is our offering for sin (Hebrews 9:22-26). Just as the priests washed daily with water in the laver, so we are made clean by Jesus through washing from the water of the Word of God (John 15:3; Ephesians 5:26). Just as the Holy Place contained the lampstand, the altar of incense, and the bread of the presence, so Jesus is the light, our Intercessor, and the bread of life feeding our hearts and souls with His very presence (John 8:12; Hebrews 7:25; John 6:35). Just as the Holy of Holies was the place where God Himself dwelt, so too, our hearts are where the triune God Himself lives.

What does the New Testament fulfillment of the Old Testament tabernacle mean for you today?

- You are a living tabernacle of God (1 Corinthians 3:16).

- The Lord Himself now lives in you (John 14:23; Romans 8:9; 2 Corinthians 6:16; Galatians 2:20).

- The Lord's presence is with you and in you at all times (Matthew 28:20; Hebrews 13:5).

- You are now joined to the Lord and one with Him (1 Corinthians 6:17-20).

- You belong to God and are to be holy, consecrated, set apart for Him (1 Peter 1:14-16).

- Just as God's glory filled the tabernacle, so His glory is now in you through the Holy Spirit. It is as though the light has been turned on inside of you, and now you shine with His brightness (2 Corinthians 3:18; 4:6-7).

While I was studying the organization of the tribes of Israel camped around the tabernacle, I noticed a design in Numbers 2 that God Himself specifically directed, outlined, and engineered. Figure 1 shows the organization of the camps around the tabernacle. Imagine that you are in an airplane looking down on the people of Israel and the tabernacle. What shape do you see? It's clear, isn't it! You see the cross.

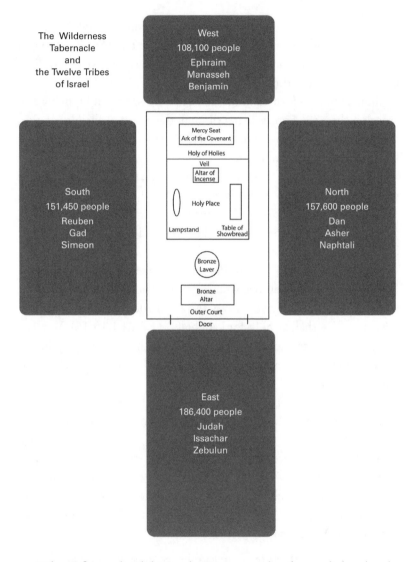

The Wilderness Tabernacle and the Twelve Tribes of Israel

West
108,100 people
Ephraim
Manasseh
Benjamin

South
151,450 people
Reuben
Gad
Simeon

North
157,600 people
Dan
Asher
Naphtali

Mercy Seat
Ark of the Covenant

Holy of Holies

Veil

Altar of Incense

Holy Place

Lampstand

Table of Showbread

Bronze Laver

Bronze Altar

Outer Court

Door

East
186,400 people
Judah
Issachar
Zebulun

When I first realized this truth, I was amazed and overwhelmed at the powerful plan of God, pointing to the cross of Christ. I thought about how those people, without even realizing it, were witnesses of redemption.

Then I thought about God looking at the earth and seeing His people in the wilderness, camped in the shape of the cross. I wondered what He must have thought, knowing about the sacrifice of Jesus on the cross for the sins of man.

Then I thought about how we are now the temple of God, living tabernacles housing the person of God through the Holy Spirit. I thought about the cross. I stood and held my arms out, and what I realized brought home the truth that the Lord now lives in us. Did you know the human body is formed in the shape of a cross? You and I, living tabernacles where the Lord is living through the power of the Holy Spirit, bear the shape of a cross. We are walking through life on earth now as living witnesses of redemption.

As you think about these truths, perhaps you feel like Jacob when he said, "Surely the LORD is in this place and I did not know it" (Genesis 28:16). What difference does God make in your life once He resides in you, His temple? The presence of Almighty God at home in your heart changes your life in several ways:

Holiness. When the God of the universe takes up residence in you, He changes the way you live your life. Peter said, "Like the Holy One who called you, be holy yourselves also in all your behavior; because it is written, 'You shall be holy, for I am holy'" (1 Peter 1:15-16). You dare not pollute the atmosphere or the air He breathes by engaging in any kind of immorality or idolatry because the God of the universe fills the temple of your life.

I recently had the opportunity to read through the memorial program celebrating the life of Dr. Henry Morris, the founder of the Institute of Creation Research. He was a humble, holy man—I know this through the firsthand experience of my friend Shirley Peters, who knew him very well for many years. What was the great secret to Dr. Morris' life? The memorial program included a page that was pasted in the flyleaf of his Bible, a challenging set of sayings entitled "Others May, You Cannot!" It quotes G.D. Watson:

> In many ways, He seems to let other good people do things which He will not let you do. Others who seem to be very religious and useful may push themselves, pull wires, and scheme to carry out their plans, but you cannot...The Lord

may let others be honored and put forward while keeping you hidden in obscurity because He wants to produce some choice, fragrant fruit for His coming glory, which can only be produced in the shade.

The indwelling Holy Spirit will lead and empower you to live out the high calling of a holy life.

Intimacy. Knowing the Lord lives in you changes your relationship with Him and the Bible. The Bible is no longer simply words on a page, but intimate instruction teaching you what He wants you to know. Knowing He lives in you changes your perspective of prayer. Prayer is no longer a ritual, but your vital conversation and communion with the one who lives in you. The result of this fellowship, this communion, this feast you have together with your Lord is intimacy. And so, "draw near to God and He will draw near to you" (James 4:8).

Ministry. I define ministry as Jesus Christ in action. In essence, Jesus lives in you and wants to change the world through you. He wants to turn this world upside down, to make you a fisher of men so that many will be saved. Jesus said that He came "to seek and save that which was lost" (Luke 19:10), and that is still His desire.

This threefold effect of the indwelling glory of God in you—Holiness, Intimacy, and Ministry—spells HIM, an acrostic reminding you to know and love the Lord.

Hudson Taylor describes a day of deep consecration:

> Well do I remember, as in unreserved consecration I put myself, my life, my friends, my all upon the altar, the deep solemnity that came over my soul with the assurance that my offering was accepted. The presence of God became unutterably real and blessed, and I well remember... stretching myself on the ground, and lying there before Him with unspeakable awe and unspeakable joy. For what service I was accepted I knew not. But a deep consciousness that I was not my own took possession of me, which has never been effaced.[1]

May you never forget the day you realized you are the temple of God and that your Lord now lives in you by the indwelling Holy Spirit.

My Response

DATE:

KEY VERSE: "Do you not know that you are a temple of God and that the Spirit of God dwells in you?" (1 Corinthians 3:16).

FOR FURTHER THOUGHT: Write a prayer of response to the Lord telling Him what it means to you that He lives in you and that you are a temple of the Holy Spirit.

MY RESPONSE:

Day Eleven

HE IS YOUR GUARANTEE OF ETERNAL LIFE

*In Him, you also, after listening to
the message of truth, the gospel of
your salvation—having also believed,
you were sealed in Him with the
Holy Spirit of promise, who is given
as a pledge of our inheritance.*

EPHESIANS 1:13-14

⤳

The Holy Spirit is the Lord's promise of your future with Him. We learn from Paul in Ephesians 1:14 that we were "sealed in Him with the Holy Spirit of promise, who is given as a pledge of our inheritance, with a view to the redemption of God's own possession, to the praise of His glory." God gives His promises to give you hope. The Holy Spirit guarantees your eternal life, your inheritance in Christ, and your redemption. And what is the immediate outcome? The praise of His glory.

D. Martyn Lloyd-Jones, the great expositor and preacher, emphasizes the immediate nature of this glory as an installment, a firstfruits, a foretaste, and an earnest of eternal glory.

It is not only a guarantee, it is a part of the thing itself. I am entering into the glory in a measure even now. Such is the Apostle's teaching. It begins here imperfectly and only in small portions; nevertheless it is real, a part of the glory itself, as much as I can stand and bear while I am still in the flesh.[1]

In Ephesians we see that the Holy Spirit is a seal and a pledge. "Seal" is a translation of the Greek word *sphragizo,* which signifies a mark of ownership and also a guarantee of authenticity. The Holy Spirit in our lives guarantees that each of us does indeed belong to God and is the real thing, the genuine article: a son or daughter of God. "Pledge" is a translation of the Greek word *arrhabon* (see 2 Corinthians 1:22; 5:5) and refers to earnest money paid beforehand to guarantee a transaction, a deposit that guarantees. The word is used figuratively here—you might even think of the Holy Spirit as the Lord's engagement ring, given to you as His promise of your future with Him. The Holy Spirit, as a pledge from God, demonstrates that there is more to come for us.

We have an inheritance with Christ in the kingdom of God. We know according to Paul in Ephesians 1:18 that this inheritance is going to be glorious. In Colossians 3:24 we see that our inheritance is our reward. Salvation is part of our inheritance (Hebrews 1:14), and it is eternal (Hebrews 9:15), imperishable, undefiled, unfading, and reserved in heaven for us (1 Peter 1:4). According to 2 Corinthians 5:1-5, we have "a house not made with hands, eternal in the heavens…our dwelling from heaven…that what is mortal will be swallowed up by life." Paul, through the Holy Spirit, expands Isaiah 64:4 to promise a glorious new future for the believer: "Things which eye has not seen and ear has not heard, and which have not entered the heart of man, all that God has prepared for those who love Him" (1 Corinthians 2:9).

You can know from the whole of Scripture that this life is not all there is, nor is it the best there is. God gives you His Holy Spirit to remind you that your real home is in heaven. Your life here on earth, walking with the Lord and filled with the Holy Spirit, is but a dim shadow of your future bright reality. "For now we see in a mirror dimly, but then face to face; now I know in part, but then I will know fully just as I also have been fully known" (1 Corinthians 13:12). Paul, who had endured earthly hardships firsthand, encouraged the suffering Philippian church that "I count all things to be loss in view of the surpassing value of knowing Christ Jesus my Lord" (Philippians 3:8). This hearkens to our earlier admonition for surrender as the key to the Spirit-filled life. If you wish to set your sail to catch the wind of the Holy Spirit, you must have the eternal perspective that earthly belongings, even earthly trials, are "but rubbish so that I may gain Christ" (Philippians 3:8). Eternal life, face-to-face with Christ, is your future.

A pastor friend of mine told me a powerful story about V. Raymond Edman, the former president of Wheaton College. Dr. Edman, at the age of 67, was speaking in the chapel at Wheaton College with my pastor friend in attendance. Dr. Edman's subject was what life will be like when we are face-to-face with the Lord. Suddenly, in the midst of one of his great declarations about eternal life, Dr. Edman collapsed.

In an instant, the Lord had taken Dr. Edman home to be with Him. He had stepped from time into eternity. In a split second, he was no longer looking "in a mirror dimly"—he was face-to-face with the Lord (1 Corinthians 13:12). He was no longer holding to the promise not yet fulfilled; he was embracing the glorious reality of always and forever being with the Lord.

My pastor friend has never forgotten what he witnessed. Indeed, I have a book by Dr. Edman entitled *But God!* and inside the front cover Dr. Edman inscribed these words: "We cannot, *but* God is able!" Raymond Edman knew the secret. And you must know it too. Dr. Edman counted on the promise and pledge of the indwelling Spirit: We are empowered in the present and secure in the future. What is your response? Live in the power of the Holy Spirit today and look forward, with all your heart, to forever—face-to-face with your Lord.

My Response

DATE:

KEY VERSE: "In Him, you also, after listening to the message of truth, the gospel of your salvation—having also believed, you were sealed in Him with the Holy Spirit of promise, who is given as a pledge of our inheritance, with a view to the redemption of God's own possession, to the praise of His glory" (Ephesians 1:13-14).

FOR FURTHER THOUGHT: What have you learned this week that you will never forget? Close today by writing a prayer to the Lord, expressing all that is on your heart.

MY RESPONSE:

QUIET TIME WEEK TWO: THE MAGNIFICENT HOLY SPIRIT

I shall ask the Father to give you someone else to stand by you, to be with you always. I mean the Spirit of truth, whom the world cannot accept, for it can neither see nor recognise that Spirit. But you recognise him, for he is with you now and will be in your hearts.

JOHN 14:15-17 PHILLIPS

PREPARE YOUR HEART

A.W. Tozer was one of those hearts on fire for the Lord this world has been privileged to know. He is the author of many Christian classics, including *The Pursuit of God* and *The Knowledge of the Holy.* Warren Wiersbe says he would wait for a new book by A.W. Tozer as impatiently "as a detective-story addict waits for the next installment of the current serial."[1] Wiersbe said he still reads his books regularly and always finds something new to think about.

A.W. Tozer was deeply spiritual. He believed that Christians could experience their faith in the depth of their being and should exist in a world of spiritual reality. He said of that kind of Christian: "He is quietly, deeply, and sometimes almost ecstatically aware of the presence of God in his own nature and in the world around him. His religious experience is something elemental, as old as time and the creation. It is immediate acquaintance with God by union with the Eternal Son."[2]

Tozer was a strong preacher of doctrine. He said that doctrine is like dynamite and must have its emphasis sharp enough to detonate before power is released. Tozer spoke and wrote often on the doctrine of the Holy Spirit. He believed that the doctrine of the Holy Spirit was "buried dynamite. Its power awaits discovery and use by the Church."[3]

As you begin your quiet time today with the Lord, ask Him to speak to you from His Word and teach you about the person and work of the Holy Spirit.

READ AND STUDY GOD'S WORD

1. Jesus promised His disciples another Comforter like Himself. Read John 14:16-18,25-26; 16:5-15 and write out everything you learn about the Holy Spirit.

2. Look at the following verses and write everything you learn about the Holy Spirit:

Acts 1:7-8

Romans 8

Galatians 5:19-26

Ephesians 5:18

3. Why do you need the Holy Spirit?

ADORE GOD IN PRAYER

> Make me, O blessed Master, strong in heart, full of courage, fearless of danger, holding pain and peril cheap when they lie in the path of duty. May I be strengthened with all might by your Spirit in my inner being.[4]
>
> F.B. MEYER

YIELD YOURSELF TO GOD

Think about these words by A.W. Tozer:

> The Holy Spirit is the Spirit of life and light and love. In His uncreated nature He is a boundless sea of fire, flowing, moving ever, performing as He moves the eternal purposes of God. Toward nature He performs one sort of work, toward the world another and toward the Church still another. And every act of His accords with the will of the Triune God. Never does He act on impulse nor move after a quick or arbitrary decision. Since He is the Spirit of the Father He feels toward His people exactly as the Father feels, so there need be on our part no sense of strangeness in His presence. He will always act like Jesus, toward sinners in compassion, toward saints in warm affection, toward human suffering in tenderest pity and love…Let us begin to think of Him to be worshipped and obeyed. Let us throw open every door and invite Him in. Let us surrender to Him every room in the temple of our hearts and insist that He enter and occupy as Lord and Master within His own dwelling…Where Christ is glorified He will move about freely, pleased and at home.[5]

ENJOY HIS PRESENCE

Have you been aware of your need for the person and power of the Holy Spirit? What is the most important truth that God has shown you in your quiet time today? Close your quiet time by writing a prayer to the Lord, expressing all that is on your heart.

REST IN HIS LOVE

"When I think of all this, I fall to my knees and pray to the Father, the Creator of everything in heaven and on earth. I pray that from his glorious, unlimited resources he will empower you with inner strength through his Spirit. Then Christ will make his home in your hearts as you trust in him. Your roots will grow down into God's love and keep you strong" (Ephesians 3:14-17 NLT).

Notes — Week Two

Week Three

THE PRESENCE OF
THE HOLY SPIRIT

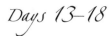

Days 13–18

HE MAKES CHRIST KNOWN TO YOU

For God, who said, "Light shall shine out of darkness," is the One who has shone in our hearts to give the Light of the knowledge of the glory of God in the face of Christ.

2 CORINTHIANS 4:6

⤳

The Holy Spirit enables you to experience the presence of Christ. You are never alone. Jesus is with you and will give you His strength. You can run to the Lord and talk with Him about everything. You can place every single need, desire, hope, and dream before Him, effectively pouring out your heart to Him. Jesus knows everything about you and longs to be intimate with you.

Are these statements just wishful thinking? No, they are the truth itself, absolute promises in the Bible, and real, personal promises for you. How are such amazing experiences of knowing Christ possible? Because of the presence of the Holy Spirit in you. The result of the indwelling Holy Spirit may be summed up in one word: *glory*. The light shining in your heart is the glory of God Himself. Paul declares, "But we all, with unveiled face, beholding as in a mirror the glory of the Lord, are being transformed into the same image from glory to glory, just as from the Lord, the Spirit" (2 Corinthians 3:18). In 2 Corinthians 4:6, he continues this thought: "For God, who said, 'Light shall shine out of darkness,' is the One who has shone in our hearts to give the Light of the knowledge of the glory of God in the face of Christ."

The Greek word *doxa* (translated "glory") refers to the splendor and radiance of God. This glory of God is the very reality of His presence in all His splendor. His glory radiates with blinding light. The amazing fact Paul reveals is that the Holy Spirit enables us to experience Christ's presence in all His splendor and glory in our own hearts. No wonder our hearts burn when Christ makes His home in us.

God in His glory is often attended by fire. The Lord spoke to Moses from a burning bush (Exodus 3:2-4), burned as fire in the cloud covering and filling the tabernacle (Exodus 40:34-38), answered by fire (1 Kings 18:24), and appeared as a radiant fire to Ezekiel (Ezekiel 1:22-28). John saw the glorified Christ as one with "eyes like a flame of fire," and "His face was like the sun shining in its strength" (Revelation 1:12-16). The brightness of the glory of God is far greater than the surface of the sun. Paul promised that if the Corinthian church thought that the glory appearing to Moses and the people of Israel was radiant, they could count on the ministry of the Holy Spirit to "be even more with glory" and "abound in glory" (2 Corinthians 3:7-11).

When John saw Christ, he "fell at his feet like a dead man" (Revelation 1:17). When you catch a glimpse of the Lord's glory, you will fall at His feet in awe and reverence. No wonder the hearts of the men on the Emmaus road burned when Jesus explained the Word of God. This same Jesus, whom John saw, now lives in you. And just as the glory filled the tabernacle, so now His glory fills you.

Perhaps the promise of God's indwelling glory is what led Paul to pray that the Ephesians would "be strengthened with power through His Spirit in the inner man, so that Christ may dwell in your hearts through faith" (Ephesians 3:16). When Jesus promised His disciples that He would give them another Comforter, He confirmed His own continuing presence with them: "If anyone loves Me, he will keep My word; and My Father will love him, and We will come to him and make Our abode with him" (John 14:23). These last words are, to me, some of the happiest, most blessed words in the entire Bible. They open up a world for us to explore. Just imagine—the triune God makes His dwelling place with us by living in us, much as He dwelled in the Old Testament tabernacle. Stop and think about this for more than a moment. This is an amazing truth that takes a lifetime to comprehend but one we must attempt to understand. Your time thinking about the indwelling of the Lord in you will pay off with countless dividends in your own life. "Christ in you" is your "hope of glory" (Colossians 1:27). Thinking about the truth of His presence in you will move your focus from outward circumstances to the inward realities of spiritual truth. Those realities will move you from perfunctory performance of religious activities to the joys of an intimate relationship with Jesus Christ as you experience Him moment by moment.

Thinking about the very real presence of Christ will help you pay attention to what the Lord is doing in and through your life. Jesus explained the work of the Holy Spirit: "He will glorify Me, for He will take of Mine and will disclose it to you" (John 16:14). The Holy Spirit will help you focus on Christ because He always glorifies Christ, drawing attention to Jesus rather than Himself. The Holy Spirit will always lead you to focus only on Christ and not on people or experiences. This magnetism to the person of Jesus distinguishes the work of the Holy Spirit in you. When you begin to look for Jesus at work in your life, the Holy Spirit will help you notice His direction. You will see the Lord's character. You will fellowship and commune with Him. This intimacy with Christ enables you to set your sail to catch the wind of the Holy Spirit.

The Holy Spirit will help you realize the truth of the indwelling Christ. "We know by this that He abides in us, by the Spirit whom He has given us" (1 John 3:24). What will you see when you experience the reality of the presence of Christ in your life? You will know, in deeper and deeper ways, who He is: His love, His joy, His peace, His patience, His kindness, His goodness, His faithfulness, His gentleness, and His self-control (Galatians 5:22-23). These are the fruit of the Spirit—the character of Jesus Christ in you. That is why Jesus said, "Abide in Me, and I in you. As the branch cannot bear fruit of itself unless it abides in the vine, so neither can you unless you abide in Me. I am the vine, you are the branches; he who abides in Me and I in him, he bears much fruit, for apart from Me you can do nothing" (John 15:4-5). "Abide" is our English translation of the Greek word *meno*, which means "to remain in vital contact." Jesus is talking about an intimate relationship, and the result is fruit, the evidence of His life in you.

One evening my husband and I were scanning through the television channels, trying to find something worthwhile to watch. We came across a fascinating portrayal of Jesus in a full-length motion picture we had never seen before: *The Visual Bible: Matthew.* We could not help but watch this presentation because we became mesmerized by this Jesus— He actually smiled, laughed, and conversed with those around Him. This was the Jesus we read about in the Bible. In many other movies, we had seen Jesus portrayed as an ethereal, untouchable being we could not identify with, certainly not someone we could talk to or laugh with, let alone trust with our salvation. That night my husband and I stayed awake for hours talking about Jesus, the Son of Man, and what He is really like as revealed in the Scriptures—an experience I would heartily recommend to everyone.

Bruce Marchiano, who portrayed Jesus in the movie, speaks of the profound impact that playing the role of Jesus had on his life. He said, "I was quite simply blown away with the unique and extraordinary experience of portraying Jesus." He shares that as he walked where Jesus walked through the events of His life, he found Jesus to be more than he had ever dreamed or hoped, and in the process, he fell even more in love with Jesus than he was before.

There is no one like Jesus. John calls Him "the One and Only" (John 1:14 NIV). Bruce Marchiano describes Jesus this way:

> Jesus—the son of a peasant girl and a laborer. Jesus—a man who didn't even have a home to call His own. Jesus—who hung out with prostitutes, thieves, cripples, and even a few fishermen. Jesus—a man who was more interested in matters of the heart than anything else. Jesus—a seemingly common, young, small-town man: sleeves rolled up, hair tossed and tumbled by a gust of first-century wind, face tanned and weathered, rough and calloused hands, dirt under the fingernails, soiled feet in well-worn sandals. Jesus—sweat

glistening on the brow, creases framing gentle eyes—eyes that look deep into your soul and inescapably breathe "I love you" with every glance. And a smile—oh, what a smile—as big as the sun, beaming at you and you alone as if you're the only person on the entire planet. *Jesus*...

Yes, Jesus smiled; yes, Jesus laughed. Jesus smiled wider and laughed heartier than any human being who has ever walked the planet. He was young. He radiated good cheer. The real Jesus was a man of such merriment, such gladness of heart, such freedom and openness, that He proved irresistible. He became known through Galilee for His genuine strength, the sparkle in His eyes, the spring in His gait, the heartiness in His laugh, the genuineness of His touch; His passion, playfulness, excitement, and vitality: His joy! He made a dazzling display of love. He set hearts afire. He was an elated, triumphant young man with an incredible quality of life...so different from the solemn religious types He constantly encountered.[1]

During Jesus' three-year public ministry, people flocked to Him and wanted Him to touch them. The desire for Jesus' touch spread throughout Galilee: "And they were bringing children to Him so that He might touch them" (Mark 10:13). "And He stretched out His hand and touched him" (Luke 5:13). "And all the people were trying to touch Him, for power was coming from Him and healing them all" (Luke 6:19). A woman who was ill saw Jesus pass by and dared to do the unthinkable—she reached out and touched the fringe of His cloak (Luke 8:43-48). Jesus responded to the woman, "Daughter, your faith has made you well; go in peace and be healed of your affliction" (Mark 5:34). When you dare to draw near and touch the hem of His garment, He responds with love and kindness. You will experience the touch of Jesus in your life through the work of the Holy Spirit. And the touch of Jesus changes your life forever.

A woman heard that Jesus was having dinner at the house of one of the religious leaders. Out of a heart of extravagant love, she brought an alabaster vial of expensive perfume and, weeping, held on to Jesus' feet, kissed them, wiped them with her hair, and anointed them with the perfume. Jesus commended this woman as one who "loved much" (Luke 7:47). Robert Murray McCheyne, known for his love of Christ through his classic *Memoirs,* speaks of this woman's act of love: "It was not the ointment Jesus cared for—what does the King of Glory care for a little ointment? But it is the loving heart, poured out upon His feet; it is the adoration, praise, love, and prayers of a believer's broken heart, that Christ cares for. The new heart is the alabaster box that Jesus loves."[2]

Do you love Jesus? Do you commune with Him? The Holy Spirit will help you experience the presence of Christ, His glory, and will always encourage you to draw near to Him. Your quiet time is the best and most profitable way to spend time with your Lord. Open the pages of the Bible to hear what He has to say to you. Talk with Him in prayer. Be still before Him to enjoy His presence. Tell Him how much you love Him.

I often think of others who had a deep, intimate relationship with the Lord. One of my favorites is Charles Spurgeon, the great preacher of the nineteenth century. Spurgeon's friend W.Y. Fullerton describes watching Spurgeon express his love for the Lord. When Spurgeon heard someone else speak about the Lord, Spurgeon would clasp his hands together and catch his breath, his eyes would fill with tears, and his face would shine with an indescribable radiance. Fullerton said that in those times, others could see the real Spurgeon, who loved the Lord Jesus Christ more than life itself.

One of the last things Spurgeon said to his wife before he passed from time into eternity was this: "Oh wifie, I have had such a blessed time with my Lord!" When you think of Spurgeon's expression of love for Christ, you cannot help but ask yourself, *What is it that delights me and gives me joy?* Will you be like those great men and women who have known and loved the Lord Jesus and find your great joy and delight in the one who loves you more than life itself? Will you be like that woman who loved Jesus with extravagant love and open the alabaster box of your heart and pour out your love for Him?

Alabaster Heart

Nothing to Thee can I bring,
Holding to Thy hand I cling.
No alabaster box have I
To break open and anoint Thee by.
I have only the heart Thou gave to me
To live, to love, to honor Thee.
Take it, my Lord, it is Thine own,
Humbly, I lay it before Thy throne.

CONNI HUDSON

My Response

DATE:

KEY VERSE: "For God, who said, 'Light shall shine out of darkness,' is the One who has shone in our hearts to give the Light of the knowledge of the glory of God in the face of Christ" (2 Corinthians 4:6).

FOR FURTHER THOUGHT: Do you know and love Jesus? In what ways have you experienced Him in your own life? What do you love most about Him? How has your reading today fueled your own desire to know and love the Lord more and experience Him in your own life?

MY RESPONSE:

HE FILLS YOU
WITH LOVE

*Hope does not disappoint, because the love of
God has been poured out within our hearts
through the Holy Spirit who was given to us.*

ROMANS 5:5

T he Holy Spirit gives you love for your enemies as well as for your
friends. This magnificent promise gives you the power not only to
forgive your enemies but also to do extravagant acts of kindness for all
the people in your life. The Holy Spirit enables you to do in love what
you cannot do alone. Paul says, "Hope does not disappoint, because the
love of God has been poured out within our hearts through the Holy
Spirit who was given to us" (Romans 5:5). The Greek word translated
"pour" is *ekcheo* and means "shed abroad and given generously." It carries with it the idea of spiritual refreshment and encouragement. The
kind of love God pours into our heart through His Holy Spirit is not
man's kind of love, *eros* or *phileo,* but God's love, *agape* love. Agape love
will renew and refresh your soul. Agape love in your heart will give you

the power to truly love your children, your husband, your friends, your family, and yes, even those who don't love you in return.

Agape love is the essential nature of God. That is why John says in 1 John 4:16 that God is love. Agape love differs from all other kinds of love. *Eros* and *phileo* love relate to the emotions and the heart, but *agape* love involves the mind and the will. Agape love is a pure affection for another that imparts value and worth, prizing and protecting that one at all costs. It is a choice, a decision, and a commitment. Agape love never gives up, always believes the best, always acts on behalf of others to meet their needs, gives at all costs—even to the death—and lasts forever. Paul describes agape love this way:

> Love is patient, love is kind and is not jealous; love does not brag and is not arrogant, does not act unbecomingly; it does not seek its own, is not provoked, does not take into account a wrong suffered, does not rejoice in unrighteousness, but rejoices with the truth; bears all things, believes all things, hopes all things, endures all things. Love never fails (1 Corinthians 13:4-8).

Imagine the difference the agape love Paul describes can make in your life and mine! If you want to know everything about agape love, look at Jesus. He loved you and me—to the death. Agape love is sufficient, infinite, unconditional, and supernatural. Let's explore these characteristics.

Agape love is sufficient. God's love does for us what we cannot do for ourselves—even providing a way for us to experience eternal life. "For God so loved the world, that He gave His only begotten Son, that whoever believes in Him shall not perish, but have eternal life" (John 3:16). God's love will not always give you what you want, but it will always give you what you need.

Once upon a time, a man became lost in his travels and wandered into a bed of quicksand. A religious leader saw the man's predicament and said, "It is evident that men should stay out of places such as this." Next, another religious leader observed the situation and said, "Let that man's plight be a lesson to the rest of the world." Another religious leader came by and said to the sinking man, "Alas, it is the will of God." Finally,

Jesus appeared. "Take my hand, brother," He said, "and I will save you."[1] Agape love sees a need and does something about it.

Agape love is infinite. Paul encouraged the Ephesian church to comprehend the breadth, length, height, and depth of Christ's love (Ephesians 3:17-19). God's love cannot be measured because it is as big as God Himself. I love Robert E. Wells' description of the dimensions of God in his classic story about the blue whale. He begins, "The largest animal on earth is the blue whale" and meanders through the ever-increasing dimensions of Mount Everest, the earth, the sun, the red giant superstar Antares, and finally the Milky Way. When you think you are impressed about the size of the Milky Way, he points to the universe:

> There are literally, *billions* of other *galaxies* in the universe. And yet, filled with billions of galaxies, the universe is almost totally empty. The distances from one galaxy to another are beyond our imagination. It defies exhaustive comprehension. And so does the One who made it! He did all that with just a spoken *word*.

God's love is immeasurable. As Paul relates, there is the sense of the infinite in the dimensions of the agape love that may "dwell in your heart through faith" (Ephesians 3:17).

Agape love is unconditional. Paul tells us, "While we were yet sinners, Christ died for us," and we were reconciled to God "while we were enemies" (Romans 5:8,10). One day while in a revival meeting, a respected missionary in China, Wiley B. Glass, ran to his missionary friend C.L. Culpepper and, in great anguish, asked his friend to pray for him. Both men went to their knees, but Glass, pale as death and groaning in his anxiety, was unable to express his agony in words. Culpepper prayed with him, and for him, several times during that day and into the next. Finally, on the evening of the second day, Glass came running to Culpepper and threw his arms around him.

"Charlie, it's gone!" Glass exclaimed.

Culpepper said, "What's gone?"

He replied, "That old root of bitterness."

Culpepper explained that 30 years earlier, before he came to China, a man had insulted his wife. The insult had made him so angry he felt he could kill the man if he ever saw him again. He realized a called servant of God should not feel that way, and his feelings had bothered him for years. Finally he released the man to God. When the Holy Spirit began working in his heart during that week, the question came, *Are you willing for that man to be saved?*

Glass answered, *Lord, I'm willing for You to save him...just keep him on the other side of heaven!* Finally, he came to the place where he said, *Lord, if that man is alive, and if I can find him when I go on furlough, I will confess my hatred to him and do my best to win him to You.* When he reached that decision, the Lord released the joys of heaven to his soul, and he was filled with love and peace. He became a more effective preacher for the Lord, and during the next few years he led hundreds to Christ. That's what the love of God poured out in the heart of man can accomplish. It is agape love, given freely with no conditions.

Agape love is supernatural. It does the unthinkable. It goes beyond the natural response of an unregenerate man and the "eye for an eye" mentality of Exodus 21:24. Rather, it seeks to be perfect as your heavenly Father is perfect (Matthew 5:48). It prays for an enemy, gives to an enemy, gives to one who desires to hurt others, gives to one who desires to hurt itself! Jesus said, "Love your enemies and pray for those who persecute you" (Matthew 5:44). But how can you, a desperate human being living alone on a desperate planet, demonstrate such a supernatural love? You can't, except through your salvation, through the power and influence of the Holy Spirit dwelling in you and directing your thoughts and actions.

Even the French romantic writer Victor Hugo, a rationalist rather than a believer, tells a story within his famous *Les Miserables* that illustrates agape love. The protagonist, Jean Valjean, is given shelter by a saintly bishop named Monseigneur Bienvenu. That very night, Valjean stole the bishop's silver cutlery and ran away. Once apprehended by the gendarmes, Valjean became dejected, knowing he was headed for prison. Monseigneur Bienvenu approached them quickly. He said to Valjean, "Ah, there you are! I'm glad to see you. But I gave you the candlesticks, too, which are silver like the rest and would bring 200 francs. Why didn't you take them along with your cutlery?" And with that, the gendarmes released Valjean to freedom. The bishop walked over to the mantel and said: "My friend, before you go away, here are your candlesticks; take them." Jean Valjean was trembling all over. "Now," said the bishop, "go in peace."

Agape love gives to thieves and prays for enemies. Now that is supernatural love, perhaps seen as outrageous, unexplainable, and inappropriate by a world mired in sin. But it is life-changing, penetrating, and purifying to the saved one of Christ who relies on the Holy Spirit for power and guidance. God relentlessly pursues you, saves you, and provides for you with His agape love. Andrew Murray summarizes God's agape love this way:

> When a three-month-old baby sleeps in his mother's arms, he lies there helplessly. He hardly knows his mother; he does not think of her, but the mother thinks of the child. And this is the blessed mystery of love: Jesus the God-man, waits to come to me in the greatness of His love, and when He gets possession of my heart, He embraces me in those divine arms and tells me, "My child, I, the Faithful One, I, the Mighty One, will remain with you. I will watch over you and keep you every day." He tells me that He will come into my heart, so that I can be a happy Christian, a holy Christian, a useful Christian.[2]

What is your response to such a love poured out by the Holy Spirit in your heart? First, receive the love of God for yourself. Bask in it. Revel in it. God loves you! He *agape* loves you! And there is no more wonderful news than to learn that God loves you. The great theologian Karl Barth was challenged by a skeptic to summarize the main theme of his theology and all that he had learned from his many years of study. He thought for a moment and then said, "Jesus loves me, this I know, for the Bible tells me so."

Second, share God's love with others. Love is active rather than passive; love is an action rather than inaction. Who in your life needs the love of God today? Will you ask God to love them in and through you?

Third, forgive your enemies. Has someone hurt you, and do you seem to be unable to forgive them? Your heart may feel hard and bitter toward them, and your basest desire may only be for revenge and retribution. In fact, your bitterness toward them is tearing your heart apart, warring with your soul. Will you bring your bitterness to God today and ask Him to replace it with His love shed abroad by His Holy Spirit? Jesus said, "A new commandment I give to you, that you love one another, even as I have loved you, that you also love one another" (John 13:34).

You can depend on the love of God in you through the Holy Spirit to enable you to do what you cannot do yourself. Spurgeon affirms this:

> There is no light in the planet but that which proceedeth from the sun; and there is no true love to Jesus in the heart but that which cometh from the Lord Jesus himself. From this overflowing fountain of the infinite love of God, all our love to God must spring...Love, then, has for its parent the love of God shed abroad in the heart.

I love thee, Lord, but with no love of mine,
For I have none to give;
I love thee, Lord; but all the love is thine,
For by thy love I live.
I am as nothing, and rejoice to be
Emptied, and lost, and swallowed up in thee.[3]

CHARLES SPURGEON

My Response

DATE:

KEY VERSE: "Hope does not disappoint, because the love of God has been poured out within our hearts through the Holy Spirit who was given to us" (Romans 5:5).

FOR FURTHER THOUGHT: How does what you read today help you understand the love of God anew in your own life? How have you experienced God's love in your own life? Who has shown you the love of God? Who needs the love of God in and through you today? What can you do to express God's love to someone else today?

MY RESPONSE:

HE REVEALS GOD'S WORD TO YOU

*Now we have received, not the spirit
of the world, but the Spirit who is
from God, so that we may know the
things freely given to us by God.*

1 Corinthians 2:12

The Holy Spirit empowers you to understand the Bible. He makes the words meaningful to you, brings them to life, and applies them to your heart. Jesus promised His disciples that when "the Spirit of truth, comes, He will guide you into all the truth" (John 16:13). The Greek word translated "guide" is *hodegeo* and carries with it the figure of one who introduces the traveler into an unknown country.[1] The Bible is an unknown country without the Holy Spirit as our travel guide. Without the Holy Spirit's illumination of the Scripture, the Bible is just so many words on a page—"foolishness" (1 Corinthians 2:14).

Think of the teaching ministry of the Holy Spirit through Paul's exhortation to the Corinthian church. The Greek word translated "know" *(oida)* means "to perceive, recognize, and understand" and is the operative word in 1 Corinthians 2:12-13. It's not a guess, not a supposition, not even intellectual imagination—it's knowing. "Now we have received, not the spirit of the world, but the Spirit who is from God, so that we may know the things freely given to us by God, which things we also speak, not in words taught by human wisdom, but in those taught by the Spirit, combining spiritual thoughts with spiritual words" (1 Corinthians 2:12-13).

God, through the work of the Holy Spirit, gave us the magnificent gift of the Bible, His Word. "But know this first of all, that no prophecy of Scripture is a matter of one's own interpretation, for no prophecy was ever made by an act of human will, but men moved by the Holy Spirit spoke from God" (2 Peter 1:20-21). Therefore, Peter encouraged believers to pay attention to the Bible as they would to a "lamp shining in a dark place" (verse 19). Paul said that "all Scripture is inspired by God and profitable for teaching, for reproof, for correction, for training in righteousness; so that the man of God may be adequate, equipped for every good work" (2 Timothy 3:16-17). The Greek word translated "inspired by God" is *theopneustos* and means "God-breathed."

The Holy Spirit, the One who authored the Bible, gives understanding and wisdom from the Word of God and makes those who give time and attention to it wiser than those who neglect the Word. The psalmist said, "O how I love Your law! It is my meditation all the day. Your commandments make me wiser than my enemies, for they are ever mine. I have more insight than all my teachers, for Your testimonies are my meditation. I understand more than the aged, because I have observed Your precepts" (Psalm 119:97-100). The writer of Hebrews shows the penetrating influence of the Bible when he says, "The word of God is living and active and sharper than any two-edged sword, and piercing as far as the division of soul and spirit, of both joints and marrow, and able to judge the thoughts and intentions of the heart" (Hebrews 4:12).

The Holy Spirit works hand in hand with the Word of God. He, the divine Author, will bring the words of the Bible to your mind either because you need them for a particular situation in your life or to teach you something important. Jesus said, "Do not worry about how or what you are to speak in your defense, or what you are to say; for the Holy Spirit will teach you in that very hour what you ought to say" (Luke

12:11-12). Have you ever been faced with a difficult situation, and suddenly a verse from the Bible came to your mind? That was the work of the Holy Spirit in you. Jesus promised, "The Holy Spirit, whom the Father will send in My name, He will teach you all things, and bring to your remembrance all that I said to you" (John 14:26). I have also experienced times when a Bible verse came to my mind, seemingly out of nowhere. When that happens, I immediately search out that verse in the Bible, study it in my quiet time, and think about its meaning for my own life. I have discovered that the more I know of the Bible, the more of God's Word the Holy Spirit can use in my life.

Do you want to know God? Do you want to know what He has to say to you? Open the pages of your Bible and read and study it. You may be thinking, *But I'm not a seminary student. I'm not a theologian.* Your understanding does not depend on you; your comprehension of God's Word depends on the Holy Spirit. He is your teacher and will make the words of the Bible come alive for you so you can understand what God is saying.

In fact, according to the Bible, no one can understand the Bible without the Holy Spirit. Spiritual things are spiritually discerned (1 Corinthians 2:14-16). Illumination by the Holy Spirit is "the ministry of the Holy Spirit whereby He enlightens those who are in a right relationship with Him to comprehend the written Word of God."[2] When you open the pages of your Bible, you can read and study confidently because the Holy Spirit is your instructor. The Holy Spirit is, according to Paul in Ephesians 1:17 (NIV), "the Spirit of wisdom and revelation."

The Bible was a mystery to me until I surrendered my life to Christ in college. After I bought a Bible, I was amazed to find verses seemingly leap off the page as though God had written them just for me. When I read Jesus' words in John 15:4-5, *"Abide in Me, and I in you...for apart from Me you can do nothing,"* I knew Jesus was saying those words directly to me. *Catherine, I want you to* "abide in Me, and I in you...for apart from Me you can do nothing." I experienced the reality of Jesus directing those words to me because of the Holy Spirit's illuminating work in my life. Opening the Bible is a thrill every day for me because of the Holy Spirit's work of making those words alive and meaningful for me. I know that every time I open the Bible, God has something to say to me. God never gives His Word without purpose. Therefore, my reading and studying of the Word is never wasted or in vain.

> For as the rain and the snow come down from heaven, and do not return there without watering the earth and making it bear and sprout, and furnishing seed to the sower and bread to the eater; so will My word be which goes forth from My mouth; it will not return to Me empty, without accomplishing what I desire, and without succeeding in the matter for which I sent it (Isaiah 55:10-11).

God's purpose in His Word is accomplished through the indwelling Spirit as He draws me to the Bible and teaches me what it means, communicating and carrying out His purpose and plan in my life.

I have always been far more interested in teaching the Word of God to people than telling them a lot of stories and illustrations and tickling their ears. Of course, I do include stories and illustrations when I speak or write—I love to tell a good story—but only to illustrate biblical truth. Our current culture encourages humorous stories and illustrations with maybe a verse from the Bible here and there. We need speakers and writers who are willing to go to God for their messages and rely on His Holy Spirit to deliver them. I think of what Paul said to the fleshly, carnal Corinthian church: "I was with you in weakness and in fear and in much trembling, and my message and my preaching were not in persuasive words of wisdom, but in demonstration of the Spirit and of power, so that your faith would not rest on the wisdom of men, but on the power of God" (1 Corinthians 2:3-5).

God's Word brought alive in your heart by the Holy Spirit will transform your life. Do you want to live for Christ? Do you want Him to set your heart on fire? Then hear what He has to say in His Word. Set aside the many things for the one thing. And the greatest thing you can do is give much time to reading and studying God's Word. No time is ever wasted in the Word of God. Your heart and soul will thank you for your time and attention to the Bible. And the Lord will set your heart on fire. Notice when the men on the road to Emmaus experienced the burning hearts—it was when Jesus was explaining the Scripture to them.

How can you read and study the Word of God? The best way is in your quiet time. Set aside a time alone with God, find a quiet place where you can draw near to Him, and use a plan for your quiet time. I like the P.R.A.Y.E.R. Quiet Time Plan that I have taught for years at retreats and conferences and that I introduced in *Six Secrets to a Powerful Quiet Time: Prepare Your Heart, Read and Study God's Word, Adore God in Prayer, Yield Yourself to God, Enjoy His Presence, and Rest in His Love.* You will find more ideas about how to incorporate devotional Bible studies into your quiet time in the 30-day journey *Knowing and Loving the Bible.* Both books are published by Harvest House Publishers.

I encourage you to find teachers who love God, know and study His Word, and walk by faith in what God says. My favorite teachers include G. Campbell Morgan, John Henry Jowett, Oswald Chambers, A.W. Tozer, Andrew Murray, Charles Spurgeon, Vance Havner, Alan Redpath, J. Edwin Orr, Amy Carmichael, Hannah Whitall Smith, and Corrie ten Boom. I read their books and listen to their sermons in MP3 format on my iPod.[3] I find their words to be clear and based on the Word of God in a generation where so few hearts beat strongly for the Lord and burn passionately for Him. These men and women challenge my commitment to the Lord and urge me to be a radical disciple for Jesus Christ, recklessly abandoned to His will.

I also encourage you to join an in-depth Bible study so you can share what God is teaching you with others who love His Word. I have been so challenged over the years by those who are committed to loving the Lord and studying His Word. I think of one Bible study leader in particular whose Bible was so marked up and worn that I sat one day and just leafed through it, amazed at her dedication to knowing God by living in His Word.

Hannah Whitall Smith speaks of her own discovery of the Bible when she first came to know Christ.

> It was all new ground to me, and I went into it with the greatest avidity. So delighted was I with the treasures I found in its pages, that at first my one fear was lest, as the Bible was such a short book, I should soon exhaust it, and come to the end of its delights, and I used to stint myself to small portions in order to spin it out the longer. But I soon found that this was not at all necessary, as the more I studied, the

more I found there was to study, and each passage seemed to have a thousand continually unfolding meanings. The book was no larger than I thought, but it was infinitely deeper. It seemed to me something as if the truths in the Bible were covered with a multitude of skins, and as if, as I studied, one skin after another was peeled off, leaving the words the same, but the meaning of those words deeper and higher.[4]

The result for Hannah Whitall Smith was a heart on fire for Jesus Christ. Hear her heart in her own words:

> It was a wonderful and delightful life I had now begun to live. I had begun to know God, and I was finding Him to be lovely and lovable beyond my fondest imaginings. The romance of my life had dawned…Then too the joy of telling it to all others, and the enormous satisfaction of seeing their faces lighten, and their hearts expand, as their souls made the same discoveries as my own…My soul had started on its voyage of discovery, and to become acquainted with God was its unalterable and unceasing aim. I was as yet only at the beginning, but what a magnificent beginning it was. God was a reality, and He was my God. He had created me, and He loved me, and all was right between us. All care about my own future destiny had been removed from my shoulders…It was no longer "How do I feel?" but always "What does God say?" And He said such delightful things, that to find them out became my supreme delight.[5]

Hannah Whitall Smith experienced devastating tragedies throughout her life, including the death of children and a difficult marriage. She wrote two important books, *The Christian's Secret of a Happy Life* and *The God of All Comfort*. Her secrets to the victorious Christian life may be traced back to her delight and love for what God says in His Word.

What a joy it is to open the pages of God's Word and draw near to God. "Your words were found and I ate them, and Your words became for me a joy and the delight of my heart; for I have been called by Your name, O LORD God of hosts" (Jeremiah 15:16). When Sir Walter Scott lay dying, he summoned to his side his man in waiting and said, "Read to me out of the Book."

"Which book?" asked his servant.

"There is only one Book," was the dying man's response—"the Bible!"

A.W. Pink says, "The Bible is the Book to live by and the Book to die by. Therefore read it to be wise, believe it to be safe, practice it to be holy." An unknown writer has said, "Know it in the head, store it in the heart, show it in the life, sow it in the world."

Have you discovered the joy and delight of the Bible? Always remember the Bible has no expiration date; a Bible in the hand is worth many more in the bookcase. When you read and study your Bible, "I pray that the eyes of your heart may be enlightened, so that you will know what is the hope of His calling, what are the riches of the glory of His inheritance in the saints" (Ephesians 1:18).

My Response

DATE:

KEY VERSE: "For who among men knows the thoughts of a man except the spirit of the man which is in him? Even so the thoughts of God no one knows except the Spirit of God. Now we have received, not the spirit of the world, but the Spirit who is from God, so that we may know the things freely given to us by God, which things we also speak, not in words taught by human wisdom, but in those taught by the Spirit, combining spiritual thoughts with spiritual words" (1 Corinthians 2:11-13).

FOR FURTHER THOUGHT: How important is the Bible in your life? What is more important to you, how you feel or what God says? Will you commit yourself to reading and studying the Bible by choosing a Bible reading plan, setting aside a time and a place, and implementing the plan for your quiet time with God? Close your time today with the Lord by writing a prayer to Him, expressing all that is on your heart.

MY RESPONSE:

HE RENEWS
YOUR HEART

*Therefore we do not lose heart, but though
our outer man is decaying, yet our inner
man is being renewed day by day.*

2 CORINTHIANS 4:16

The Holy Spirit renews your heart and soul day by day. "Therefore we do not lose heart, but though our outer man is decaying, yet our inner man is being renewed day by day" (2 Corinthians 4:16). Paul reveals to us that the Holy Spirit works in the "inner man": "[May He] grant you, according to the riches of His glory, to be strengthened with power through His Spirit in the inner man" (Ephesians 3:16). The Greek word translated "renew" is *anakainoo* and refers to a new strength and vigor, a qualitatively new kind of life, and a new beginning. Other translations render *anakainoo* as receiving "fresh strength" (Phillips) and "being made stronger" (CEV).

In these words from Paul, we see something we all have experienced—the body is wasting away. We live in a fleshly body that experiences illness and, with age, wrinkles and withers away. When I was just a teenager, a little girl looked at my eyes and remarked, "You have wrinkles under your eyes." I was only 13 and was, of course, quite startled. My mother told me that the lines under my eyes came from my big smile and that they are "crinkles," not wrinkles. Her encouraging words eased my mind then, and I choose to think of them as crinkles even today.

I realized the temporary nature of our body's health in a new way this year when I received the diagnosis of skin cancer that could leave me with possible facial scars and even disfigurement. I had to undergo a painful six-week skin treatment. When people saw me with a bandage on my face, they immediately asked me what was wrong. I responded with a smile and said, "My outer man is decaying, yet my inner man is being renewed day by day."

I learned something very important from my painful experience: Real life is inside us, in our hearts, where we know and love God. Our inner person, our spiritual self, is very much alive because we know Christ. Regardless of what you suffer, regardless of your appearance, even if you have a devastating disfigurement or disability, real life is found within. The Holy Spirit makes you strong and brand-new on the inside day by day. The outer body may be all crinkles while within, through the power and filling of the Holy Spirit, you are spiritually more alive, more vigorous, and younger than ever before.

My friend Shirley Peters just celebrated her eightieth birthday. I heard her say that the Lord showed her a verse when she turned 50—"So teach us to number our days, that we may present to You a heart of wisdom" (Psalm 90:12). She said she can hardly believe more than 30 years have passed since she found that verse. Shirley is one of the most alive people I know. She knows the Bible better than just about anyone I've met. She may not walk as quickly as she did 30 years ago, but her spirit is more vigorous and stronger than ever before.

Always remember, every day is a new day with the Holy Spirit at work in your heart. He wants to give you new vigor and strength in every area of your life. He wants to renew your mind: "And do not be conformed to this world, but be transformed by the renewing of your mind" (Romans 12:2). The Holy Spirit changes the way you think by helping you think on what is true, honorable, right, pure, lovely, of good repute, excellent, and worthy of praise (Philippians 4:8). The Holy

Spirit gives you a new day-by-day experience of intimacy and knowledge of the Lord. You "have put on the new self who is being renewed to a true knowledge according to the image of the One who created him" (Colossians 3:10).

Some Bible commentators believe Paul spoke about inner renewal by the Spirit because the fleshly, carnal Corinthian church was looking at him only outwardly, observing his aging appearance, which was affected by much suffering and persecution.

> Others may only see a withered, crushed apostle, pounded by overwhelming hardships. If they do not look at him with the eyes of faith, they will not see the real Paul on a portrait locked away in heaven that is ever being transformed into the likeness of Christ. As his outward life conforms ever more closely to the crucified Christ, his inward life conforms ever more closely to the glorified Christ.[1]

> But it is a secret process, invisible both to the outsider and to the believer himself, known only to faith. To protect that faith from the encroachments of pride, which would turn spiritual renewal into a human achievement instead of accepting it as a gift of grace, God has provided that the process be concealed within an "earthenware vessel," a perishable body subject to pain and decay (2 Corinthians 4:7; 12:7-9). Those whose eyes are not on the seen and transient, but on the unseen and eternal, can detect beneath the decay of the outer nature an inner life which is being daily renewed (2 Corinthians 4:16-18).[2]

Will you today choose to focus on your life that is "hidden with Christ in God" (Colossians 3:3)? Continually "set your mind on the things above, not on the things that are on the earth" (verse 2). Count on the promise of inner renewal by the Holy Spirit when you are faced with earthly sorrow and decay, regardless of the adversity or heartbreak. Louis Blériot, the French aviator who in 1909 became the first person to fly across the English Channel, was forced to use crutches as the result of an accident. While approaching his airplane to make the record-setting flight, he remarked to his companions, "I cannot walk, but I can fly." May our inner self always "mount up with wings like eagles" in the power of the Holy Spirit (Isaiah 40:31).

My Wings

I cannot walk, but I can fly;
No roof can house me from the stars,
No dwelling pen me in its bounds,
Nor keep me fast with locks and bars;
No narrow room my thoughts can cage,
No fetters hold my roving mind;
From these four walls that shut me in
My soaring soul a way can find.

With books and pictures at my side
All lands, all ages, are my own;
I dwell among the master minds,
The best and greatest earth has known;
I flee to strange and storied scenes
Of long ago and far away,
And roam where saints and heroes trod
In Time's forgotten Yesterday.

With every wandering butterfly
Or singing bird on vagrant wing
My fancy takes the airy trail,
And follows it, adventuring,
Till higher than their highest flight,
Where cloud-ships drift and star-beams shine,
I rise on tireless pinions fleet,
And all the realms of space are mine.

From out the paling sunset skies
The Twilight Angels come to me
On dusky wings to bear me swift
To shadowy haunts of Memory
Where, 'mid the gardens and the graves,
I wander, smiling through my tears,
With all the dear and deathless dead.
The loved and lost of vanished years.

And, when the long, long day is done,
I clasp the dearest Book of all
And through the dim, sweet silences
I hear my Father's accents fall;
Then, though in chains, yet am I free.
Beyond the pressure of my care,
Above Earth's night my spirit mounts
On eagle wings of faith and prayer.[3]

ANNIE JOHNSON FLINT

My Response

DATE:

KEY VERSE: "Therefore we do not lose heart, but though our outer man is decaying, yet our inner man is being renewed day by day" (2 Corinthians 4:16).

FOR FURTHER THOUGHT: Where in your life do you need the inner renewal of the Holy Spirit? Write a prayer to the Lord asking Him for that renewal today.

MY RESPONSE:

Day Seventeen

HE SETS YOUR HEART FREE

Now the Lord is the Spirit, and where
the Spirit of the Lord is, there is liberty.

2 CORINTHIANS 3:17

⤷

The Holy Spirit gives you freedom to live as a child of God. "There is therefore now no condemnation for those who are in Christ Jesus. For the law of the Spirit of life in Christ Jesus has set you free from the law of sin and death...set free from its slavery to corruption into the freedom of the glory of the children of God" (Romans 8:1-2,21).

What does this kind of freedom mean for you? Your freedom begins as a judicial freedom whereby the judge has declared you forgiven. "He made you alive together with Him, having forgiven us all our transgressions, having canceled out the certificate of debt consisting of decrees against us, which was hostile to us; and He has taken it out of the way, having nailed it to the cross" (Colossians 2:13-14).

Your freedom then becomes real in your experience in the same way a prisoner enjoys life outside prison walls when he is set free. The only difference is that you never paid the price for your sin; Jesus paid it for you.

"And He died for all, so that they who live might no longer live for themselves, but for Him who died and rose again on their behalf...Therefore if anyone is in Christ, he is a new creature; the old things passed away; behold, new things have come" (2 Corinthians 5:15,17). The result of all that Jesus did is freedom for you. The indwelling Spirit makes this freedom real in your life. "Now the Lord is the Spirit, and where the Spirit of the Lord is, there is liberty" (2 Corinthians 3:17).

You no longer live by a religion of rules but are free to enjoy a relationship with convictions. "For the kingdom of God is not eating and drinking, but righteousness and peace and joy in the Holy Spirit" (Romans 14:17). You are free to live as a child of God would live. You don't live in the gutter of this world, alone and helpless; rather, your home is with God Himself. That is why Paul said, "Set your mind on things above, not on the things that are on earth. For you have died and your life is hidden with Christ in God. When Christ, who is our life, is revealed, then you also will be revealed with Him in glory" (Colossians 3:2-4).

Because you are free, you can say yes to life with the Lord and no to those things that would displease Him. Paul describes our life this way: "Therefore, we also have as our ambition, whether at home or absent, to be pleasing to Him" (2 Corinthians 5:9). When you enjoy a relationship with your Lord, you will form certain convictions, commitments, and resolves through the leading of the Holy Spirit because you love Him.

Your freedom does not mean you are free to sin. "For you were called to freedom, brethren; only do not turn your freedom into an opportunity for the flesh, but through love serve one another" (Galatians 5:13). Paul continues by encouraging the Galatians to "walk by the Spirit, and you will not carry out the desire of the flesh" (verse 16). When you are filled with the Spirit, the Spirit is in control of your life. The filling of the Spirit enables you to say yes to God and no to the works of the flesh: "immorality, impurity, sensuality, idolatry, sorcery, enmities, strife, jealousy, outbursts of anger, disputes, dissensions, factions, envy, drunkenness, and carousing" (verses 19-21).

When you are walking by the Spirit, you confess your sin when He convicts you of wrongdoing. Then you yield yourself to God through surrender, giving way to His ways, and ask Him to fill you with His

Holy Spirit again. Bill Bright, in *The Holy Spirit,* calls this continuous day-by-day action "spiritual breathing"—exhaling by confession of sin and inhaling by asking for the filling of the Holy Spirit. These actions are by faith and are based on the promises of God's Word for forgiveness of sins (1 John 1:9), the filling of the Holy Spirit (Ephesians 5:18), and answered prayer (1 John 5:14-15). Your faith is not in your feelings, but in the promises of God's Word.

When you live with a heart set free, you learn that "not all things are profitable" (1 Corinthians 6:12) and "not all things edify" (1 Corinthians 10:23). The Holy Spirit gives you liberty to love, not license to sin. You will begin, by the work of the Holy Spirit in you, to live a life of love for God, who lives in you, and for others who live with you (Galatians 5:13). In love, you will set aside your own rights and choose never to do anything that would cause another to stumble. And because of your love for God, you live the life you were meant to live, enjoying fellowship with Him. "Those who live to please the Spirit will harvest everlasting life from the Spirit" (Galatians 6:8 NLT).

A heart set free is a heart set on fire for Christ. Richard Halverson is a great example of a heart set on fire for Jesus Christ. For 20 years, Richard Halverson had no interest in God. In fact, he aspired to success in the field of entertainment. At the age of 19, he went to Hollywood. After six months of careless living and financial difficulty, he went to a nearby church, looking for answers. Three months later he became a Christian. Through his new relationship with Christ, his ambitions changed, and he realized that God had a definite plan for his life that involved evangelism, missions, or pastoral ministry. His heart was now set free.

Following a profound surrender to Christ at Mt. Hermon Christian Conference Center, Halverson attended seminary at Wheaton College and then pastored a church in Coalinga, California. There in Coalinga, the Holy Spirit brought him to a deeper commitment to Christ and a willingness to live in obscurity if that was what the Lord desired.

One month later, Halverson attended a training conference at the Forest Home Christian Conference Center in the San Bernardino mountains. Following an evening meeting, he made his way back to his cabin, passing the cabin of Henrietta Mears, founder of Forest Home. Though her cabin was darkened, he realized some inside were praying.

"I was strangely constrained to enter and pray...so I opened the door, crossed the room through the darkness...I began to pray, others followed, and God came down into that cabin." There was weeping and laughter, much talking and planning, God laying a burden for the world on those souls.

Halverson finally got back to his cabin in the middle of the night, sat down at his typewriter, and wrote what later became known as the four commitments of the Fellowship of the Burning Heart. The four commitments encompassed the essentials of a dedicated Christian life: devotion, holiness, evangelism, and surrender. Halverson sealed these commitments with this statement: "God being my guide I desire to make these commitments to HIM." Halverson shared these commitments with Henrietta Mears and those who had attended the cabin prayer session, thus forming the Fellowship of the Burning Heart for that era.

Oh, how the Lord used Richard Halverson. He became pastor of the Fourth Presbyterian Church in Bethesda, Maryland, and later became chaplain of the United States Senate from 1981 to 1994. His love for Jesus Christ became known to the world. He once said, "Jesus Christ is God's everything for man's total need." That is the statement of one whose heart is on fire for Jesus Christ. May his tribe increase.

My Response

DATE:

KEY VERSE: "Now the Lord is the Spirit, and where the Spirit of the Lord is, there is liberty" (2 Corinthians 3:17).

FOR FURTHER THOUGHT: How has the Lord spoken to your heart today? Will you draw near to Him now and pray about your own commitment and resolve to live for Christ?

MY RESPONSE:

Day Eighteen

QUIET TIME WEEK THREE: CHRIST LIVES IN YOU

Those who obey God's commandments remain in fellowship with him, and he with them. And we know he lives in us because the Spirit he gave us lives in us.

1 JOHN 3:24 NLT

PREPARE YOUR HEART

Andrew Murray was a minister, speaker at the Keswick convention, and author of numerous books on the Christian life. His book *With Christ in the School of Prayer* was instrumental in the Welsh Revival when Reverend Joseph Jenkins read it and was profoundly convicted about the importance of obedience to the Holy Spirit. One of his most well-known books focused on the life of Christ in man: *Abide in Christ*. One of the most powerful truths the Holy Spirit teaches you is the fact that Christ now lives in you. He is not just with you, but in you. This truth radically changes everything about your life: You are never alone again, and you can always talk with your Lord and commune with Him.

As you begin your quiet time today, ask the Lord to open the eyes of your heart.

READ AND STUDY GOD'S WORD

1. We learn from John that Christ lives in us through the indwelling Holy Spirit. Read the following verses and write everything you learn about Christ in you:

    John 14:20

    John 14:23

    Galatians 2:20

    Colossians 1:27

    1 John 3:24

2. Read John 15:1-9 and write out everything you learn about abiding in Christ. The Greek word translated "abide" is *meno* and in this context means to "remain in vital contact with Jesus Christ."

3. What will help you remain in vital contact with (abide in) Jesus?

ADORE GOD IN PRAYER

Pray the following prayer by Amy Carmichael:

My heart said unto Thee:
My face would seek Thy face:
O Lord, grant me this grace:
Shine down on me.

Myself would cloud my skies.
Let self be crucified;
Let love be fortified;
Anoint mine eyes.

Thee would I see and know;
All else would I forget.
Let Thy fair beauty set
My life aglow.[1]

YIELD YOURSELF TO GOD

Meditate on these words about abiding in the vine by Andrew Murray:

God is in all. God dwells in Christ. Christ lives in God. We are in Christ. Christ is in us: our life taken up into His; His life received into ours. In a divine reality that words cannot express, we are in Him and He is in us. And the words "Abide in Me and I in you" just tell us to believe in this divine mystery. We are to count on our God the Husbandman, and Christ the Vine, to make it divinely true. No thinking or teaching or praying can grasp it—it is a divine mystery of love. As little as we can influence the relationship, can we understand it. Let us just look upon this infinite, divine, omnipotent Vine loving us, holding us, working in us. Let us, in the faith of His working, abide and rest in Him, ever turning heart and hope to Him alone. And let us count on Him to fulfill in us the mystery: "You in Me, and I in you."

Blessed Lord, You bid me to abide in You. How can I abide, Lord, except by Your showing Yourself to me, waiting to receive and welcome and keep me? I ask You to show me how You, as Vine, undertake to do all. To be occupied with You is to abide in You. Here I am, Lord, a branch, cleansed and abiding—resting in You, and awaiting an inflow of Your life and grace.[2]

ENJOY HIS PRESENCE

Christ lives in you by the power of the Holy Spirit. Describe in your own words what that means to you today. How does His presence in your life encourage you?

REST IN HIS LOVE

My old self has been crucified with Christ. It is no longer I who live, but Christ lives in me. So I live in this earthly body by trusting in the Son of God, who loved me and gave himself for me (Galatians 2:20 NLT).

Notes — Week Three

Week Four

THE POWER OF
THE HOLY SPIRIT

Days 19–24

Day Nineteen

POWER FOR PERSONAL REVIVAL

*"He who believes in Me, as the Scripture
said, 'From his innermost being will
flow rivers of living water.'" But this
He spoke of the Spirit, whom those who
believed in Him were to receive.*

JOHN 7:38-39

≫

You will experience personal spiritual revival by the power of the Holy Spirit. Abundant overflowing life is possible because of the Holy Spirit at work in you. Jesus gave us this promise: "'If anyone is thirsty, let him come to Me and drink. He who believes in Me, as the Scripture said, "From his innermost being will flow rivers of living water."' But this He spoke of the Spirit, whom those who believed in Him were to receive" (John 7:37-39). We must respond to the invitation of Jesus every day of our lives until we are face-to-face with Him in eternity. We depend on those rivers of living water in our lives on a daily basis because of sin, suffering, and our need for spiritual growth.

One early morning many years ago, spent from a long speaking trip, I opened my Bible to find that my reading for the day was Psalm 119. I thought, *Oh no! I really don't want to read this psalm today because it's so long, and I already know this psalm is all about the Word of God. I've studied it before many times.* I stared at the page and took a large gulp of coffee, allowing my eyes to scan down the 176 verses. Suddenly, as I was reading, I saw something I had not seen before. I noticed a word repeated many times throughout that psalm—*revive. That's new,* I thought, still waking up. *Well, of course it isn't new,* I chided myself. *The Lord is trying to get my attention!* The Lord had compelled me to stop and live in Psalm 119 that day. I met with God that morning, and my quiet time in Psalm 119 altered the course of my life.

The Lord sometimes brings a verse or a word from the Bible to my mind, and I have learned to wake up, pay attention, and listen for His teaching from His Word. Every day for the next couple of weeks, I kept reading and thinking about Psalm 119 in my quiet time. I discovered that Psalm 119 was an "orphan psalm"—a prayer to the Lord by someone (perhaps Ezra) whose heart and soul were in trouble. "I lie in the dust; revive me by your word" (verse 25 NLT). "I weep with sorrow; encourage me by your word" (verse 28 TLB). "I am shriveled like a wineskin in the smoke…" (verse 83 NLT).

Have you ever felt that way? Spiritually dried and shriveled up? Prompted by his profound distress, the psalmist's prayer was highly personal—revive *me.* The word *revive* is repeated 11 times throughout Psalm 119:

- Revive me according to Your word (25).

- Revive me in Your ways (37).

- Revive me through Your righteousness (40).

- Your Word has revived me (50).

- Revive me according to Your lovingkindness (88).

- You have revived me (93).

- Revive me, O LORD, according to Your word (107).

- Revive me, O Lord (149).

- Revive Me according to Your word (154).

• Revive me according to Your ordinances (156).

• Revive me, O LORD, according to Your loving-kindness (159).

Over and over again in Psalm 119, revive me, revive me, revive me! I thought, *Something about this word* revive *is significant and must be very important to God.* As a result of my time in Psalm 119, at the inception of Quiet Time Ministries, I began to study revival. I can truly say that my quiet times in Psalm 119 have altered the course of my life, and I ultimately wrote a book of quiet times entitled *Revive My Heart!*

Do you know what I learned? I learned that the revival referred to most frequently in the Bible is personal, spiritual revival. It's personal—revive *me,* O Lord. It's spiritual—*revive* me, O Lord. The psalmist's heart and soul needed reviving. The Hebrew word translated "revive," *chayah,* implies a quickening of heart and soul imparting whatever is necessary to sustain one's spiritual life and enable a return to the experience of one's true purpose as ordained by God.

In revival, God restores you so He can carry out His plans and purposes in your life. Without personal spiritual revival on a daily basis, we wallow in sin, despair in suffering, and never experience spiritual growth.

Jesus depicts the work of the Holy Spirit as rivers of living water flowing from our innermost being. This flow of the Holy Spirit provides the life-giving river of personal revival necessary to restore us to God's plan and purpose for our life. Every day we are faced with temptations. Every day we are faced with trials. And every day we are faced with the need for transformation. The Holy Spirit is faithful to convict us so we can confess our sin and be restored to fellowship with Christ (1 John 1:9). The Holy Spirit is faithful to comfort our hearts in the midst of painful adversity (Acts 9:31). The Holy Spirit is faithful to transform our hearts, moment by moment, making us more and more like Christ (2 Corinthians 3:17-18). These rivers of living water flowing from the Holy Spirit are rivers of restoration, renewal and refreshing, providing just what we need when we need it. The Holy Spirit gives us the experience of the reality of the presence of Christ, His glory. And we learn that "times of refreshing may come from the presence of the Lord" (Acts 3:19).

When the rivers of revival are flowing from your innermost being, dear friend, you will move from sin to holiness, discouragement to joy, and complacency to spiritual growth. I think often of the story of young King Josiah (2 Kings 22) ascending the throne at the tender age of eight years. Josiah "did right in the sight of the Lord and walked in all the way of his father David" (2 Kings 22:2). But by the age of 18, he was forced to address the necessity for revival within his kingdom and wisely ordered the repair of the house of the Lord. The priest found the book of the law, and Shaphan, the scribe, read it to the king. When Josiah heard the words of God and realized their truth, he literally tore his clothes, utterly stunned by the disobedience of the people and their complete disregard for God's Word.

He "tore his clothes"—that is the key phrase pointing toward revival. Ancient Near-Eastern people tore their clothes as an expression of deep sorrow and remorse.[1] Reuben, remorseful for throwing his brother Joseph into the pit, "tore his garments" (Genesis 37:29). David rent his garments when he heard that Absalom had slain his brothers (2 Samuel 13:31). And Hezekiah, faced with the invasion of Judah by the Assyrians, tore his clothes, praying for deliverance from the Lord (2 Kings 9:1,15). As Brian H. Edwards summarizes, "The men God uses in revival were always men who did not merely pay lip-service to the authority of Scripture. They had a fear of being disobedient. This was the key factor in the reformation under Josiah."[2] In this regard, Josiah may be considered the last godly king of Judah, personally and spiritually revived by God and instrumental in the revival of his people. Revival begins when "the sinner begins to inquire, 'What must I do to be saved?'"[3]

"Go inquire of the LORD," exclaimed King Josiah, "for great is the wrath of the LORD that burns against us" (2 Kings 22:13). Thus, Josiah commanded the priest to go to God and inquire what must be done because the people had ignored the Word of God. The Lord said to Josiah, "Because your heart was tender and you humbled yourself before the LORD when you heard what I spoke...and you have torn your clothes and wept before Me, I truly have heard you" (verse 19). Josiah's response was to make "a covenant before the LORD, to walk after the LORD, and to keep His commandments and His testimonies and His statutes with all his heart and all his soul" (23:3). Josiah's heart had been set on fire, and as a result, all the people of his kingdom entered into the covenant of

Josiah. Josiah, setting his sail to catch the wind of the Holy Spirit, ordered revolutionary reforms, demolishing the idols the people had built for themselves and commanding that the people celebrate Passover.

Transformation occurs when personal, spiritual revival takes place in the heart of an individual as it did in Josiah. Do you know what God thought about Josiah? "Before him there was no king like him who turned to the LORD with all his heart and with all his soul and with all his might, according to the law of Moses; nor did any like him arise after him" (2 Kings 23:25). May we be like a Josiah in our generation who will turn to the Lord with all of our heart and soul and might and drink freely and fully of Him that we too may experience the rivers of living water flowing from our innermost being.

My Response

DATE:

KEY VERSE: " 'If anyone is thirsty, let him come to Me and drink. He who believes in Me, as the Scripture said, "From his innermost being will flow rivers of living water." ' But this He spoke of the Spirit, whom those who believed in Him were to receive" (John 7:37-39).

FOR FURTHER THOUGHT: Describe what personal, spiritual revival is and how you may experience it. What meant the most to you from the life of Josiah? What was your favorite insight from this day of reading? In what ways can you see the Holy Spirit at work in your life in the areas of temptation, trials, and transformation?

MY RESPONSE:

POWER FOR MINISTRY

*Now there are varieties of gifts, but the
same Spirit. And there are varieties of
ministries, and the same Lord. There
are varieties of effects, but the same God
who works all things in all persons. But
to each one is given the manifestation
of the Spirit for the common good.*

1 CORINTHIANS 12:4-7

The Holy Spirit gives you everything you need to carry out your ministry. Paul himself declared, "I can do all things through [Christ] who strengthens me" (Philippians 4:13). The Lord is the one who does the work of ministry, not us. In essence, ministry is Jesus Christ in action. Paul teaches about God's gifts, ministries, and effects, and we see them functioning in others throughout the Bible.

"Now there are varieties of gifts, but the same Spirit. And there are varieties of ministries, and the same Lord. There are varieties of effects, but the same God who works all things in all persons" (1 Corinthians

12:4-7). Notice the emphasis on "the same Spirit," "the same Lord," and "the same God." The triune God is at work in and through us to accomplish His plans and purposes. God also emphasizes "varieties" (the Greek word is *diairesis*), implying great diversity. For example, Billy Graham's gift of evangelism was carried out in his crusade ministry and resulted in thousands of people experiencing the effect of salvation. God accomplishes His will by gifting us, raising up various ministries, and bringing about His desired results.

Oswald Chambers is one of my heroes of the faith. I know him through the devotional *My Utmost for His Highest,* which I have used in my quiet time for more than 30 years. His insights and exhortations have challenged me to walk closely with my Lord. I admire his fervent commitment and devotion to Christ. You may not know that Oswald Chambers lived only 43 years, dying tragically of a ruptured appendix while ministering in Cairo, Egypt. Although he wrote only one book, *Baffled to Fight Better,* more than 30 books have his name as the author. How can this be?

His wife, Biddy, a gifted court stenographer, transcribed all of Oswald Chambers' messages in shorthand during their seven years of marriage. After his death, she spent the next 50 years compiling books from her shorthand notes. Biddy and Oswald Chambers illustrate for us how God gifts people, appoints them for ministry, and then produces the desired effect. Oswald Chambers had no idea how God would use his wife to carry on a powerful ministry of writing and organizing material to produce books. And neither one of them could have possibly imagined the profound effect of the little devotional Biddy compiled of Oswald Chambers' messages, which she titled *My Utmost for His Highest.* This Christian classic has been continuously in print in the United States since 1935 and remains in the top ten titles of religious book bestseller lists with millions of copies in print.

Be assured, if you know Jesus Christ, you are gifted for ministry, you will be led into a ministry, and your ministry will have a certain effect brought about by God Himself. Every Christian has at least one spiritual gift, but no Christian exercises all the gifts at once. "But to each one is given the manifestation of the Spirit for the common good" (1 Corinthians 12:7) and "for the equipping of the saints for the work of service, to the building up of the body of Christ" (Ephesians 4:12). However, all Christians have all of the Holy Spirit, who distributes gifts when and where they are needed.

The Holy Spirit is your divine enablement; when you are filled with the Spirit, you are empowered for ministry. The gifts described in the Bible include these: prophecy, miracles, healing, tongues, evangelism, pastor-teacher, teacher, service, helps, faith, exhortation (encouragement), discernment, mercy, giving, administration, wisdom, and knowledge (Romans 12:6-8; 1 Corinthians 12; 14; Ephesians 4:11-12). A "gift" (Greek: *charisma*) is a divine endowment of a special ability for service within the body of Christ. God gives spiritual gifts so you can carry out the work of the Lord.

How can you know how God has gifted you? First, be filled with the Holy Spirit. Your desires will fall in line with your spiritual gifts when you are filled with the Spirit rather than living a fleshly life. Secondly, learn about the spiritual gifts listed in the Bible (see appendix 3 for a more detailed description of spiritual gifts). Become involved in ministries that interest you within the church. I have found that the best way to discover your spiritual gifts is to begin to serve in ministry. Begin right where you are in the church where God has led you. You will soon discover those areas where God has gifted you. He will lead and guide you into ministry. He designed you. He has placed you on this earth for a reason. You are here by His design. The real secret to discovering your spiritual gifts is saying, *Lord, I am available, anytime and anywhere.* Your spiritual gifts will become apparent.

Always remember that the Lord will lead you on His journey for you—what I like to call a pilgrimage of the heart. God may lead you to difficult areas of ministry in order to train you for His higher purposes. Spiritual maturity and ministry development take time and rigorous training. My own journey with the Lord has included seasons when I did not like His chosen course, and I have had years when I felt I was on the shelf in total obscurity. And yet, in both instances, I was exactly where God wanted me. Those times brought me to deeper commitments to my Lord. Was I willing to serve Him even if there was no applause? Was I willing to do whatever He asked even if those things were not my first choice? You see, God makes us who we need to be so we can do what

He calls us to do. I could never sit for hours alone and write the books God has asked me to write had I not learned the faithfulness of serving Him in the obscure years of the past.

The great perspective of ministry is that Jesus is doing His work in and through you. You are never alone in ministry—you are working together with the Lord Jesus Christ. Paul served with this same perspective. He said he was "working together with Him" in 2 Corinthians 6:1 and called his group "God's fellow workers" in 1 Corinthians 3:9. Working together with the Lord Jesus Christ is a perspective based on reality. After the resurrection of Christ and His ascension into heaven, the disciples "went out and preached everywhere, while the Lord worked with them" (Mark 16:20). If He worked with His disciples then, He continues to work with us as His disciples now. And He accomplishes His work through the power of the Holy Spirit.

You should always serve in ministry out of love for Christ. Charles Spurgeon affirms this thought: "Love should give wings to the feet of service, and strength to the arms of labor. Fixed on God with a constancy that is not to be shaken, resolute to honor him with a determination that is not to be turned aside, and pressing on with an ardor never to be wearied, let us manifest the constraints of love to Jesus."[1] This statement is made in the context of his vast ministry.

Ray Stedman, author and former pastor of Peninsula Bible Church, speaks of the difference between ministry in the flesh and ministry in the Spirit. He says that the mark of a fleshly ministry is that as soon as the attention fades, it quits. Then he describes the alternative:

> The mark of the ministry of the Spirit is that, regardless of whether anyone says anything or sees anything, it keeps right on going! That is because it is unto the Lord. You can't continue with the perennial enthusiasm that you show without having discovered the secret of resting on the indwelling life of Jesus Christ. That is why this wholehearted, continual service is the mark of a Spirit-filled ministry.[2]

Ask yourself whether your ministry meets the Spirit-filled criteria of wholehearted, continual service? If not, dear friend, reset your sail to catch the wind of the Holy Spirit, changing the course of your ministry.

When you serve the Lord in the power of the Holy Spirit, exercising your gifts and serving in the ministries He has given you, whether large or small, you will experience a sense of awe (Acts 2:43). You will see the Lord do God-sized things, things only He could possibly accomplish. You will be in awe of Him as you watch Him take the little that you do and make something amazing happen. You will worship Him for who He is and what He does. You may see some of the results now, but only heaven will tell the real story of what God has done in and through you as you have faithfully walked with Him and served Him moment by moment. May He receive all the glory for the life you live in the power of His Spirit while here on earth.

My Response

DATE:

KEY VERSE: "Now there are varieties of gifts, but the same Spirit. And there are varieties of ministries, and the same Lord. There are varieties of effects, but the same God who works all things in all persons. But to each one is given the manifestation of the Spirit for the common good" (1 Corinthians 12:4-7).

FOR FURTHER THOUGHT: How have you experienced the power of the Holy Spirit while serving the Lord in ministry? How has God gifted you in ministry? What ideas has He placed in your heart for ministry?

MY RESPONSE:

Day Twenty-One

POWER FOR DIFFICULT CIRCUMSTANCES

Finally, be strong in the Lord and in the strength of His might.

EPHESIANS 6:10

≫

The Holy Spirit will give you strength in trials and difficult circumstances. When you experience trials and tribulations, you will be tempted to rely on your own miniscule strength. But God wants you to rely on His strength, from the Holy Spirit in you, in the very heat of the trial. Paul's imperative is this: "Finally, be strong in the Lord and in the strength of His might" (Ephesians 6:10).

You have an arsenal of strength available to you in the Lord through the indwelling Holy Spirit. The Greek word translated "strong" is *endunamoo* and means "to be equipped, strengthened, and empowered." You are to find this equipping, strength, and empowering in the Lord and His mighty power and ability. The "strength of His might" is, according to Paul, the same power that raised Jesus from the dead (Ephesians 1:19-21). Paul prayed that the church at Ephesus would know "the surpassing greatness" of God's power on their behalf (verse 19). You need to know that God is able, and He has every resource and capability to handle whatever comes your way. The secret to victory in difficulties will always be finding your strength in the Lord and not in yourself regardless of how strong you think you are.

D. Martyn Lloyd-Jones, in his classic commentary on Ephesians, says this:

> Start by reminding yourself of His strength. Look at Him, he [Paul] says, look at His power. You have been looking at the enemy and you have seen his strength; you have looked at yourself and you are trembling in your weakness and in your ineffectiveness; well now, he says, look at Him, "Be strong in the Lord." To be "strong in the Lord" you must remember "the might of his power," "the might of his strength." Express it whichever way you like, but look at Him and realize all the reserves of strength and power that are in him.[1]

When you are in a difficult place, squeezed in on every side, turn your attention away from your circumstance and look to the character and person of your Lord. Cry out to God in prayer and tell Him about your specific trouble. Be like Mary, the mother of Jesus, when she came to Him and simply laid out the problem at hand: "They have no wine" (John 2:3). Be like David, who said, "Give ear to my words, O LORD, consider my groaning. Heed the sound of my cry for help...In the morning, O LORD, You will hear my voice; in the morning I will order my prayer to You and eagerly watch" (Psalm 5:1-3). Be like King Hezekiah, who spread his trouble out before the Lord (2 Kings 19:14). When you give God your trouble, you can tell Him what you would like, but you should never presume to tell Him what He should do. Prayer is not commanding God, but asking and seeking Him with the knowledge that He can accomplish what has probably never even entered your mind.

Then open your Bible, meditate on His Word, and let your mind dwell on who God is and what He can do. You might live in one of the great books on the character and attributes of God such as *Knowing God* by J.I. Packer or *The Knowledge of the Holy* by A.W. Tozer. One of my favorite promises about God's character is Ephesians 3:20: "Now to

Him who is able to do far more abundantly beyond all that we ask or think, according to the power that works within us…" The Greek word translated "power" there is *dunamis,* the same word used in Acts 1:8 and that refers to the power of the Holy Spirit that gives you everything you need for every circumstance of life. William Gurnall, in his classic *The Christian in Complete Armour,* says this: "In the army of saints, the strength of the whole host lies in the Lord of hosts. God can overcome His enemies without help from anyone, but His saints cannot so much as defend the smallest outpost without His strong arm."[2]

You are a soldier in the army of the Lord. Always remember to use the equipment the Lord has given you for the battles you face. Every battle includes a spiritual warfare, according to God's Word: "For our struggle is not against flesh and blood, but against the rulers, against the powers, against the world forces of this darkness, against the spiritual forces of wickedness in the heavenly places" (Ephesians 6:12). We learn from Paul in verse 11 that we must stand firm against "the schemes of the devil."

The enemy we face is the devil himself, and he is, according to Peter, prowling around "like a roaring lion, seeking someone to devour" (1 Peter 5:8). Peter speaks of the devil in the context of times of suffering and anxiety, and says that we must cast all our anxiety on the Lord because He cares for us. Then we can resist the devil, firm in our faith (verses 7,9). You will experience spiritual warfare most often in times of suffering. You will be tempted to despair and give up entirely. We see this in the lives of the disciples: "We were burdened excessively, beyond our strength, so that we despaired even of life" (2 Corinthians 1:8). In times of discouragement, draw on the power and strength of the Holy Spirit. In times of trouble, you will be tempted to move away from what you know is true, honorable, right, pure, lovely, of good repute, excellent, and worthy of praise (Philippians 4:8). You will be tempted to worry, become discouraged, or even panic. And you will try to draw on your own limited resources. This is a losing game plan (verses 6-7).

I have experienced failure when I have drawn upon my own limited resources. When I ran to God, at the first hint of a trial, and trusted what He said in His Word, I found renewed strength to live the life He had planned for me along with peace of mind. I remember years ago when I needed a job, any job, so that my family could have enough money to survive. I could not seem to find work anywhere. I was shocked at the difficulty of finding a job because I was a fast typist and very good on the computer. I thought I would be hired right away.

I ran to the Lord and asked Him to lead me, guide me, and show me what to do. I received the idea to try getting hired through a temporary employment agency. I took a typing test and finally was hired as a receptionist at an accounting firm. This was quite a step back for me considering I had a master's degree in theological studies and had been an office manager in a medical practice. I had hired people to do what I was now doing. The spiritual warfare was now heating up within me. What would I believe—that God had a plan for me or that life as I knew it was over?

I believe the greatest part of every battle is the fight of faith in our own hearts and minds. Perhaps that is why Paul told his disciple, Timothy, to "fight the good fight of faith" (1 Timothy 6:12). I think the enemy would have loved for me to give up on God and fall into despair. In my own fight of faith, I found the strength I needed in my quiet time with the Lord. Every day I found new promises in the Bible to hold on to as I struggled with my limited perspective of the circumstances in my life. The Holy Spirit applied the Word of God to my heart, helping me to focus on my relationship with the Lord. And in fact, the Holy Spirit is our strength in the heat of the battle, and His offensive weapon is "the sword of the Spirit, which is the word of God" (Ephesians 6:17). Living in the Bible, the Word of God, every day is essential to your life, for its words are your offensive weapon and will enable you to stand firm when trials and difficulties assail you on every side.

I do not think God was as concerned about where I was working as He was about where I was abiding. He wanted me to find life in Him, not in what I did for Him. He was showing me that life is a pilgrimage of the heart where I find my home more and more in Him. I literally took His words to my heart day by day in my quiet time, and moment by moment I found joy in Him.

I remember being asked to file a large stack of accounting charts. I looked at that filing job and said to the Lord, *If You want me to file accounting charts for the rest of my life, I am going to do it in Your strength and power and find joy in You even in this task.* I filed those charts in the joy of the Lord and found Him to be my strength even in the most menial of tasks. Life is not about what you do, but about who you know and who loves you.

Years later, I am now writing books and speaking at retreats and conferences as part of Quiet Time Ministries. These responsibilities require exactly what I learned in that emergency job as a receptionist: a focus on life in the Lord and His Word and not on what I do for a living. Perhaps the Lord will ask me to do something brand-new tomorrow. Life can change for any of us with the snap of a finger—we must learn to find our strength in God, not in ourselves or in favorable circumstances.

Paul instructs us in Ephesians 6:13 to "take up the full armor of God." The armor of God is spiritual and will enable you to resist the devil. Our duty is to stand firm because the battle, in fact, is the Lord's. "The battle is the LORD's" was David's war cry when he prepared to fight the giant Goliath (1 Samuel 17:47). He was not interested in wearing earthly armor, even the king's armor. He knew that the Lord was his strength.

Our spiritual armor includes truth, righteousness, the gospel of peace, faith, and salvation. Ask God to put the belt of truth around your waist, the breastplate of righteousness over your heart, the gospel of peace on your feet, the shield of faith all around you to "extinguish the flaming arrows of the evil one," and the helmet of salvation for your mind. Then, hang on to the Word of God with all that is in you, for it is the sword that the Spirit will use to fight the battle.

Jesus provided the finest example of using the Word of God offensively when He was tempted by the devil following 40 days and 40 nights in the wilderness. He answered everything the devil sent His way with one theme: what God said in His Word. "It is written, 'Man shall not live on bread alone, but on every word that proceeds out of the mouth of God'…It is written, 'You shall not put the Lord your God to the test'…It is written, 'You shall worship the Lord Your God, and serve Him only'" (Matthew 4:4-10). Three times, Jesus said, "It is written." You must do the same. Can you see the importance of your time in the Word of God, especially in spiritual warfare? Your quiet time builds up your spiritual ammunition to prepare you for spiritual battles.

In spiritual warfare, you must also wield another great offensive weapon: prayer. "With all prayer and petition pray at all times in the Spirit" (Ephesians 6:18). When you lay out your requests before God, the enemy has nothing to say. The enemy roars with a deafening blast to try to make you afraid and run, but always remember, "Greater is He who is in you than He who is in the world" (1 John 4:4). Humility and brokenness are the prerequisites to the kind of fervent prayer that brings every desire before the Lord. God gives strength to those who are humble and broken (1 Peter 5:6-7). Often the difficult circumstances are what humble and break us, enabling us to easily turn our dependence and trust to the Lord, who has the very strength we need. The psalmist discovered this great secret: "O Lord, you have heard the desire of the humble; You will strengthen their heart, You will incline Your ear" (Psalm 10:17). God promises that He will strengthen your heart—anchor you, so you cannot be moved—when you lay out your desire before Him.

God, by the power of the Holy Spirit in you, is sufficient for whatever trial you might face in life. He is the Father of mercies and the God of all comfort (2 Corinthians 1:3). I have a dear friend named Conni who is in the heat of a physical battle and lives with chronic pain. I have watched the Lord give her the strength to continue studying the Word, serving Him, and running the race He has set before her. Her dependence on God encourages me to draw near and depend on Him as well. As you depend on God and experience His power in your present difficulty, you will become a strong witness and encouragement to those around you.

Martin Luther found his encouragement in perilous times in the strength and power of the Lord. One of his favorite psalms was Psalm 46, and one of his favorite verses was, "God is our refuge and strength, a very present help in trouble." He wrote the beloved hymn "A Mighty Fortress Is Our God" from those words, and it became the battle cry of the Protestant Reformation. May it become your battle cry as well.

A mighty fortress is our God,
A bulwark never failing;
Our helper He amid the flood
Of mortal ills prevailing.
For still our ancient foe
Doth seek to work us woe—

His craft and power are great,
And, armed with cruel hate,
On earth is not His equal.

Did we in our own strength confide,
Our striving would be losing,
Were not the right man on our side,
The man of God's own choosing.
Dost ask who that may be?
Christ Jesus, it is He—
Lord Sabaoth His name,
From age to age the same,
And He must win the battle.

And though this world, with devils filled,
Should threaten to undo us,
We will not fear, for God hath willed
His truth to triumph through us.
The prince of darkness grim,
We tremble not for him—
His rage we can endure,
For lo! his doom is sure:
One little word shall fell him.

That word above all earthly powers,
No thanks to them, abideth;
The Spirit and the gifts are ours
Through Him who with us sideth.
Let goods and kindred go,
This mortal life also—
The body they may kill;
God's truth abideth still:
His kingdom is forever.

My Response

DATE:

KEY VERSE: "Finally, be strong in the Lord and in the strength of His might" (Ephesians 6:10).

FOR FURTHER THOUGHT: What is your difficulty today? Will you take your difficulty to the Lord, lay it out before Him, and then ask Him to fight your battle? Write a prayer to the Lord, expressing all that is on your heart. You might want to turn to Ephesians 6:10-18 and pray through those words, asking the Lord to clothe you completely with His full spiritual armor.

MY RESPONSE:

POWER FOR PRAYER

*In the same way the Spirit also helps our
weakness; for we do not know how to pray as
we should, but the Spirit Himself intercedes
for us with groanings too deep for words.*

ROMANS 8:26

The Holy Spirit is your strength in prayer. Even when you do not
know what to pray, you can rely on the Holy Spirit, for He knows
the will of God. "In the same way the Spirit also helps our weakness; for
we do not know how to pray as we should, but the Spirit Himself intercedes for us with groanings too deep for words; and He who searches
the hearts knows what the mind of the Spirit is, because He intercedes
for the saints according to the will of God" (Romans 8:26-27). What an
encouragement this is for you when you pray to the Lord.

Prayer is your great privilege as a child of God. Because of your adop-
tion by God as His son or daughter, you may cry out to Him, "Abba!
Father!" (Romans 8:15). You may call on God the same way Jesus did
in the Garden of Gethsemane when His soul was deeply grieved: "Abba!
Father! All things are possible for You; remove this cup from Me; yet not

what I will, but what You will" (Mark 14:36). The phrase "Abba! Father!" is an intimate family expression of Aramaic origin and means "My Father, my dear father." *Abba* is an affectionate word, similar to *Daddy* or *Papa*.

Paul expands on this phrase in Galatians 4:6-7: "Because you are sons, God has sent forth the Spirit of His Son into our hearts, crying, 'Abba! Father!' Therefore you are no longer a slave, but a son; and if a son, then an heir through God." You can approach God with absolute confidence and delight in prayer knowing that you are now family and are afforded the same privilege as Jesus in addressing your Father with this most intimate expression, "Abba! Father!" The writer of Hebrews confirms this boldness when he says, "For we do not have a high priest who cannot sympathize with our weaknesses, but One who has been tempted in all things as we are, yet without sin. Therefore let us draw near with confidence to the throne of grace, so that we may receive mercy and find grace to help in time of need" (Hebrews 4:15-16).

The Holy Spirit not only enables us to cry out "Abba! Father!" but also intercedes on our behalf. The Spirit's role of intercession is seen in the meaning of the word *huperentugchano*. It is "a picturesque word of rescue by one who 'happens on' another who is in trouble and 'in his behalf' pleads with 'unuttered groanings' or 'sighs that baffle words.'"[1] When we are so troubled that we cannot speak, we know the Holy Spirit is speaking on our behalf without our having to utter any actual words. And God hears what the Holy Spirit says even in our abject silence because when God searches our hearts, He hears all that the Spirit says. And what the Spirit says is "according to the will of God" (Romans 8:27). You can be encouraged, dear friend, to know that in your deepest, darkest times, when you draw near to God, you cannot go wrong in prayer when you rely on the prayer of the Holy Spirit on your behalf.

John Hyde, often called "Praying Hyde" by his contemporaries at the turn of the twentieth century, was known for the anointing of the Holy Spirit in prayer. An American evangelist of the same era, Dr. J. Wilbur Chapman, speaks of his own experience praying with John Hyde. He had asked Hyde to pray for him, and Chapman describes the event:

> He came to my room, turned the key in the door, dropped
> on his knees, waited five minutes without a single syllable

coming from his lips. I could hear my own heart thumping and beating. I felt the hot tears running down my face. I knew I was with God. Then with upturned face, down which the tears were streaming, he said: "Oh, God!" Then for five minutes at least, he was still again, and then when he knew he was walking with God his arm went around my shoulder and there came up from the depth of his heart such petitions for men as I had never heard before. I rose from my knees to know what real prayer was.

Hyde's goal was to take Chapman into the presence of God in the power of the Holy Spirit, and he did. In contrast, when Peter began sinking into the water, he cried out only, "Lord, save me" (Matthew 14:30). Nothing more, nothing less. Whether simple or complex, concise or labored, reserved or passionate, the key to real prayer is the power of the indwelling Holy Spirit. Real Spirit-driven prayer cries out to God.

How can you discover what real prayer is? How can you pray with power? Begin by praying to be filled with the Holy Spirit. Pray through the Word of God, verse by verse and line by line. Read books on prayer and practice what God teaches you. Be bold and courageous in prayer, like the psalmist who said, "I love the LORD because He hears my voice and my supplications. Because He has inclined His ear to me, therefore I shall call upon Him as long as I live" (Psalm 116:1-2). Draw near to the Lord today, cry out "Abba! Father!" and rely on God, through the power of the Holy Spirit within you, to help you talk with Him in prayer.

My Response

DATE:

KEY VERSE: "In the same way the Spirit also helps our weakness; for we do not know how to pray as we should, but the Spirit Himself intercedes for us with groanings too deep for words; and He who searches the hearts knows what the mind of the Spirit is, because He intercedes for the saints according to the will of God" (Romans 8:26-27).

FOR FURTHER THOUGHT: What is the most important truth you learned about prayer and the Holy Spirit today? Close your time by pouring out your heart in prayer to the Lord today and begin by crying out, "Abba! Father!"

MY RESPONSE:

Day Twenty-Three

POWER FOR WITNESSING

You shall be My witnesses.

ACTS 1:8

≫

The Holy Spirit gives you power to witness for the Lord. In fact, Jesus does not want you to witness for Him without the power of the Holy Spirit. He told His disciples to stay in the city until they were "clothed with power from on high" (Luke 24:48-49). Jesus wants you to be clothed with the power of the Holy Spirit so you can tell all who will listen who He is and how they can know Him. He said to His disciples just prior to His ascension, "You will receive power when the Holy Spirit has come upon you; and you shall be My witnesses both in Jerusalem, and in all Judea and Samaria, and even to the remotest part of the earth" (Acts 1:8).

The power of the Holy Spirit gives you supernatural boldness to share the gospel of Jesus Christ. Many years ago in St. Louis, a lawyer visited a Christian to transact some business. Before the two parted, his client said to him, "I've often wanted to ask you a question, but I've been afraid to do so."

"What do you want to know?" asked the lawyer.

The man replied, "I've wondered why you're not a Christian."

The man hung his head, "I know enough about the Bible to realize that it says no drunkard can enter the kingdom of God, and you know my weakness!"

"You're avoiding my question," continued the believer.

"Well, truthfully, I can't recall anyone ever explaining how to become a Christian."

Picking up a Bible, the client read some passages showing that all are under condemnation but that Christ came to save the lost by dying on the cross for their sins. "By receiving Him as your Substitute and Redeemer," he said, "you can be forgiven. If you're willing to receive Jesus, let's pray together."

The lawyer agreed, and when it was his turn he exclaimed, "O Jesus, I am a slave to drink. One of your servants has shown me how to be saved. O God, forgive my sins and help me overcome the power of this terrible habit in my life." Right then and there he was converted. The converted attorney's name was C.I. Scofield, who later became the illustrious editor of the Scofield Reference Bible that bears his name.

The power of the Holy Spirit gives you a supernatural joy and satisfaction in witnessing. C.T. Studd, a famous cricket player who became a Christian and later a missionary in India and Africa in the 1800s, said, God "set me to work for Him, and I began to try and persuade my friends to read the Gospel, and to speak to them individually about their souls…I cannot tell you what joy it gave me to bring the first soul to the Lord Jesus Christ. I have tasted almost all the pleasures that this world can give…but those pleasures were as nothing compared to the joy that the saving of that one soul gave me." C.T. Studd used to exclaim: "Some wish to live within the sound of church or chapel bell; I want to run a rescue shop within a yard of hell."

The power of the Holy Spirit gives you a supernatural wisdom in witnessing. He will give you the words to say and then show you what to do. One of the greatest obstacles to witnessing is the fear that you will not know what to say. Jesus promised His disciples wisdom in speaking even in their most desperate hour: "Do not worry about how or what you are to say; for it will be given you in that hour what you are to say. For it is not you who speak, but it is the Spirit of your Father who speaks in you" (Matthew 10:19-20). I often think about the man who was brave enough to share the gospel with Charles Colson. He gave Colson a copy of the book *Mere Christianity*. Colson read it and became a Christian.

The power of the Holy Spirit gives you supernatural results in witnessing. Never underestimate what God may want to do through you. A couple of years ago I had the great privilege to attend a Billy Graham crusade on a Friday evening in San Diego. I had never heard or seen Billy Graham live, and I knew this would probably be my one and only opportunity. What an experience! I was moved to tears by George Beverly Shea singing his classic "I'd Rather Have Jesus." And then Billy Graham came to the stage, helped to the podium by his son, Franklin Graham. I felt very humbled and privileged to finally hear one of my heroes in the faith in person. He shared from the parable of the prodigal son. It was a simple yet profound message.

He closed with a powerful illustration about a young man who very much wanted a car for his high school graduation. He let his father know exactly which car and how much it cost. When the time came for him to receive his gift from his father, much to his disappointment, his father handed him a small package. He opened it to discover a Bible. The son was so angry at the gift that he threw the Bible to the ground, left the house, and never spoke to his father again. Many years passed, and the day came when his father died. The son received the news and went home to be with his mother for the funeral. When he got home, he went into the living room, and there he saw the Bible his father had given him for high school graduation so many years ago. He picked it up and began leafing through it. When he got to the end, he saw something fluttering from the back page. He looked more closely, and there, taped to the last page, was a certified check in the exact amount of the car he had wanted.

After Billy Graham shared that story, he then said to the crowd of thousands in attendance, *now* is the time of decision. Don't wait until it is too late! But before Graham even finished giving his invitation, people began pouring out of the stands to come down on the field. Not just hundreds of people, but thousands. I was astounded at the response. I have never seen anything like it—it was a great movement of the Holy Spirit. Someone put a chair behind the podium so Billy Graham could sit down as he waited for thousands to come to the field so he could pray with them.

Imagine this scene for yourself. On the large screen was a projected image of a humble Billy Graham sitting down, resting, his head bowed in prayer. As you looked around the stadium, thousands of people were pouring out of the stands and coming forward to give their lives to Jesus Christ. Do you know what the lesson was to me? Jesus was doing the work, not Billy Graham or any other person. There was only one at work—the Lord Jesus moving up and down those aisles and drawing hearts to Himself. Finally, Billy Graham stood to pray with these people. But hundreds were still standing in line in the aisles, trying to get down to the field. He began to pray. Those standing in line were praying out loud with him. What an electrifying movement of the Holy Spirit.

I remember hearing Billy Graham interviewed on Larry King's CNN interview program. Larry King asked him why God had chosen him to do the great work of evangelistic crusades and to impact so many people. Billy Graham responded, "I have no idea why." It was so clear to me as I experienced this crusade firsthand that witnessing is God's work through and through. Never underestimate what God can do in and through the lives of those who are wholly yielded to Him! I love C.T. Studd's quote: "Only one life will soon be past, only what's done for Christ will last!" "But thanks be to God, who always leads us in triumph in Christ, and manifests through us the sweet aroma of the knowledge of Him in every place" (2 Corinthians 2:14).

The Lord doesn't call us all to be a Billy Graham or to conduct evangelistic crusades. However, the Lord does expect us to give a clear presentation of the gospel in the power of the Holy Spirit to any who will hear. When you share the gospel with someone and are filled with the Holy Spirit, you can know God is at work. Sometimes you are called to sow the seed of the truth of Christ, and other times you have the privilege of reaping the harvest and praying with someone to receive Christ.

How can you become a faithful witness in the power of the Holy Spirit? First, learn how to share the gospel. I like to use the Four Spiritual

Laws, published by Campus Crusade for Christ. Learn the four main points of the gospel:

- God loves you and has a wonderful plan for your life (John 3:16).

- Man is sinful and separated from God; therefore, he cannot know and experience God's love and plan (Romans 3:23; 6:23).

- Jesus Christ is God's only provision for man's sin. Through Him you can know and experience God's love and plan for your life (John 14:6; Romans 5:6-8).

- We must individually receive Jesus Christ as Savior and Lord; then we can know and experience God's love and plan (John 1:12; Acts 16:30-31; Romans 10:13; Revelation 3:20).

You may lead people in a prayer like this: *Lord Jesus, I need You. Thank You for dying on the cross for my sins. I open the door of my life and receive You as my Lord and Savior. Thank You for Your forgiveness and the gift of eternal life. Take control of my life and make me the person You want me to be, in Jesus' name. Amen.*

Second, ask God to give you opportunities to share the gospel with others. "Conduct yourselves with wisdom toward outsiders, making the most of the opportunity. Let your speech always be with grace, as though seasoned with salt, so that you will know how you should respond to each person" (Colossians 4:5-6). One of the best ways to begin sharing the gospel with someone is to tell them your own story of salvation. This is your testimony. Write out how you came to know Christ as a three-minute testimony. Memorize it so you can feel the freedom to share your story as the Lord gives opportunity, anytime, anywhere. Always remember, no meeting is by chance. The Lord is the author of divine appointments.

Two young Christian women set out from Portland, Oregon, to go on a much-needed weekend vacation. They drove toward the Oregon coast, not knowing exactly which beachside town would be their final destination. They came to a fork in the road requiring a quick decision. They decided to turn left. While on their way to the little beachside town, they spoke together of their need to grow in their quiet time with the Lord. They arrived one hour later and saw a sign to the Cannon Beach Christian Conference Center. They decided to investigate their blessing and asked if they could rent a room.

The attendant replied, "Yes, but only if you attend the women's conference here this weekend."

They asked, "What is the topic?"

The woman replied, "Quiet time, and the speaker is Catherine Martin of Quiet Time Ministries." Those women knew that it was no accident they had arrived in Cannon Beach and that God had orchestrated their weekend for His purposes.

God is the author of divine appointments. Bill Bright used to say, "Although I have shared Christ personally with many thousands of people through the years, I am a rather reserved person, and I do not always find it easy to witness. But I have made this my practice, and I urge you to do the same: Assume that whenever you are alone with another person for more than a few moments, you are there by divine appointment to explain to that person the love and forgiveness he can know through faith in Jesus Christ." Keep your eyes open for God's opportunities to share His love with others who need to know Him.

I'd Rather Have Jesus

I'd rather have Jesus than silver or gold;
I'd rather be His than have riches untold;
I'd rather have Jesus than houses or land;
I'd rather be led by His nail-pierced hand:

Than to be the king of a vast domain
Or be held in sin's dread sway!
I'd rather have Jesus than anything
This world affords today.

I'd rather have Jesus than men's applause;
I'd rather be faithful to His dear cause;
I'd rather have Jesus than world-wide fame;
I'd rather be true to His holy name.

RHEA F. MILLER

My Response

DATE:

KEY VERSE: "You will receive power when the Holy Spirit has come upon you; and you shall be My witnesses both in Jerusalem, and in all Judea and Samaria, and even to the remotest part of the earth" (Acts 1:8).

FOR FURTHER THOUGHT: What encourages you the most to share your faith with someone else? How did you come to know the Lord? What is your story? Will you learn how to share your faith and then make the most of every opportunity to share it in the power of the Holy Spirit?

MY RESPONSE:

Day Twenty-Four

QUIET TIME
WEEK FOUR:
I CAN'T, BUT HE CAN!

*[May He] grant you, according to the
riches of His glory, to be strengthened
with power through His Spirit in the
inner man, so that Christ may dwell
in your hearts through faith.*

EPHESIANS 3:16

PREPARE YOUR HEART

The cry of the Christian filled with the Holy Spirit is always "I can't,
but He can!" John Henry Jowett learned this valuable spiritual truth early
in his preaching ministry when he was overwhelmed by his new responsibilities. He had trained for the ministry but was young and had accepted
the pulpit of a well-known church whose former pastor had died. The
pressure to perform was heavily laid on Jowett, and many thought he
would not be up to the task. Knowing the power of God and His calling to great tasks, Jowett trusted the Lord and studied the Word with all
diligence. God honored his heart and empowered Jowett to become one
of the greatest preachers in the English-speaking world. He received as
many as 30 invitations a day to preach. He wrote numerous books that
are treasures in rich devotional reading.

As you begin your time with the Lord, ask God to show you how His power will make a difference in how you live your life.

READ AND STUDY GOD'S WORD

1. Paul prayed a very important prayer for the church at Ephesus. Read this prayer (Ephesians 3:14-21) in the following translations, underlining the phrases and words that are most significant to you:

> For this reason I bow my knees before the Father, from whom every family in heaven and on earth derives its name, that He would grant you, according to the riches of His glory, to be strengthened with power through His Spirit in the inner man, so that Christ may dwell in your hearts through faith; and that you, being rooted and grounded in love, may be able to comprehend with all the saints what is the breadth and length and height and depth, and to know the love of Christ which surpasses knowledge, that you may be filled up to all the fullness of God. Now to Him who is able to do far more abundantly beyond all that we ask or think, according to the power that works within us, to Him be the glory in the church and in Christ Jesus to all generations forever and ever. Amen (NASB).

> When I think of all this, I fall to my knees and pray to the Father, the Creator of everything in heaven and on earth. I pray that from his glorious, unlimited resources he will empower you with inner strength through his Spirit. Then Christ will make his home in your hearts as you trust in him. Your roots will grow down into God's love and keep you strong. And may you have the power to understand, as all God's people should, how wide, how long, how high, and how deep his love is. May you experience the love of Christ, though it is too great to understand fully. Then you will be made complete with all the fullness of life and power that comes from God. Now all glory to God, who is able, through his mighty power at work within us, to accomplish infinitely more than we might ask or think. Glory to him in the church and in Christ Jesus through all generations forever and ever! Amen (NLT).

2. What phrase or word from Ephesians 3:15-21 means the most to you today?

3. Read the following verses and record what you learn about the power and strength of the Lord in your life:

Romans 8:11

2 Corinthians 3:4-5

2 Corinthians 12:7-10

Philippians 4:13

ADORE GOD IN PRAYER

Pray through and meditate on the words of this prayer by F.B. Meyer:

> Father of Jesus, give me that same Holy Spirit, who raised him from the dead, that he may raise me also. I long that his risen life may be more evidently mine, and that I may experience the power of his resurrection, rising as a fountain in my soul.[1]

YIELD YOURSELF TO GOD

The power flows up, and out and over! It is a spring, and therefore incalculable. We can measure the resources of a cistern; we can tell its capacity to a trifle. We can register the contents of a reservoir; at any moment we can tell how many gallons it contains. But who can measure the resources of a spring? It is to this spring-like quality in the Divine power, the exceeding abundance, the immeasurable quantity, that the apostle refers. We can bring our little vessels to the spring and take them away filled to overflowing, and the exceeding abundance remains. The "doing" of our God is an inexhaustible well.

"Above all we ask." The ability of God is beyond our prayers, beyond our largest prayers…what I have asked for is as nothing compared to the ability of my God to give. I have asked for a cupful, and the ocean remains! I have asked for a sunbeam, and the sun abides! My best asking falls immeasurably short of my Father's giving. It is beyond all that we can ask…When all our workings and all our thinkings are put together, and piled one upon another, like some stupendous Alpine height, the ability of our God towers above all, reaching away into the mists of the immeasurable.[2]

JOHN HENRY JOWETT

ENJOY HIS PRESENCE

Where in your life do you need the immeasurable power of God today? Will you draw near and ask the Lord to do what only He can do in your life?

REST IN HIS LOVE

"I am ready for anything through the strength of the one who lives within me" (Philippians 4:13 PHILLIPS).

Notes — Week Four

Week Five

THE PURPOSE OF
THE HOLY SPIRIT

Days 25–30

Day Twenty-Five

HE MAKES YOU
LIKE CHRIST

*But we all, with unveiled face, beholding as
in a mirror the glory of the Lord, are being
transformed into the same image from glory
to glory, just as from the Lord, the Spirit.*

2 CORINTHIANS 3:18

The Holy Spirit transforms you inwardly, making you like Christ. How can the old character become new? How can a bad person become good? How can a slave trader become a hymn writer? How can a thief become a philanthropist? Transformation of your inner being from unholiness to the holiness of Christ—sanctification—is only made possible by the Holy Spirit, both positionally and experientially.

Paul spoke of this inner change as both a completed masterpiece (positional) and a continual process (experiential). Second Corinthians 5:17 emphasizes the completed work of sanctification with this phrase: "If anyone is in Christ, he is a new creature; the old things passed away, behold, new things have come." Second Corinthians 3:18 reveals the ongoing nature of sanctification: "But we all, with unveiled face, beholding as in a mirror the glory of the Lord, are being transformed into the same image from glory to glory, just as from the Lord, the Spirit." The Greek word *metamorphoo* (translated "transformed") refers to a change of condition and form. It is the same word used for the Lord's transfiguration in Mark 9:2 when "He was transfigured...and His garments became radiant." This type of transformation reminds us of the metamorphosis of a caterpillar into a butterfly—you are not a minor alteration of the old person, but you become someone completely brand-new.

Your inner change—sanctification—is the fulfillment of the New Covenant promise in Jeremiah 31:33-34:

> "I will put My law within them, and on their heart I will write it; and I will be their God and they shall be My people. They will not teach again, each man his neighbor and each man his brother, saying, 'Know the LORD,' for they will all know Me from the least of them to the greatest of them," declares the LORD, "for I will forgive their iniquity, and their sin I will remember no more."

And the New Covenant becomes manifest by the work of the Holy Spirit: "For the law of the Spirit of life in Christ Jesus has set you free from the law of sin and of death" (Romans 8:2). In essence, the Holy Spirit brings about an inner change and does in you what you cannot do for yourself. This process of sanctification is a multifaceted experience.

The Holy Spirit enables you to know Christ practically rather than hypothetically. Part of the Holy Spirit's transformation process is giving you knowledge of Christ. "We all attain to the unity of the faith, and of the knowledge of the Son of God" (Ephesians 4:13). This knowledge is not an academic acquiring of facts about Him, but an intimate, personal relationship with Him. You will know how He thinks and how He acts. Just the other day, in my quiet time, I read John 10 about the Lord as my good Shepherd and realized again His watchful care over me, helping me compassionately counsel a woman in distress over her marriage relationship.

The Holy Spirit enables you to experience the reality and splendor of Christ's presence. This is known as the "glory of the Lord" (2 Corinthians 3:18). He is not remote and distant, but intimate and alive in you.

According to Paul, the experience of Christ's presence within is an ongoing process of growth as you move from glory to glory. What you experience today is only the beginning of something that becomes more incredible until the day you see your Lord face-to-face. I vividly remember lying on a table in an emergency room after a head-on motor vehicle accident in Dallas, Texas. As the physician was injecting a local anesthetic into my scalp wounds, I suddenly remembered the Lord's crown of thorns and immediately sensed His presence with me.

The Holy Spirit enables you to become like Christ. This inner transformation gives you the character of Christ. Paul spoke to the Galatians of his fervent desire for them to be Christlike when he proclaimed, "I am again in labor until Christ is formed in you" (Galatians 4:19). How is Christ formed in us? You can now know Christ personally, so in a very real sense you "see" Him. You are "beholding as in a mirror the glory of the Lord." When you see Him, you become like Him. In fact, John tells us that "now we are children of God, and it has not appeared as yet what we will be. We know that when He appears, we will be like Him, because we will see Him just as He is" (1 John 3:2).

What will you look like in real life now? More and more, you will look like Jesus. His beauty will shine through you. What has happened in you will become apparent in your actions, and you will love others like Jesus. "Love one another, even as I have loved you...by this all men will know that you are My disciples, if you have love for one another" (John 13:34-35). You will experience His joy: "These things I have spoken to you so that my joy may be in you, and that your joy may be made full" (John 15:11). You will know His peace: "Peace I leave with you; My peace I give to you; not as the world gives do I give you. Do not let your heart be troubled, nor let it be fearful" (John 14:27). These changes are not theoretical plausibilities but objective realities in your own life, produced by the work of the Holy Spirit in you. Paul says that we have "put on the new self who is being renewed to a true knowledge according to the image of the One who created him" (Colossians 3:10).

The Holy Spirit enables you to become spiritually mature. The Holy Spirit works in you, through the process of sanctification, the ability to move from spiritual childhood to spiritual maturity. Paul encouraged the Ephesians to become mature in the faith...

> to the stature which belongs to the fullness of Christ. As a
> result, we are no longer to be children, tossed here and there
> by waves and carried about by every wind of doctrine, by
> the trickery of men, by craftiness in deceitful scheming; but
> speaking the truth in love, we are to grow up in all aspects
> into Him who is the head, even Christ (Ephesians 4:13-15).

Early in my relationship with Christ, I was challenged by some members of a religious cult on my college campus. Their beliefs startled and confused me. I was forced to examine the Bible for myself, and through the power of the Holy Spirit, I discovered what I believed. My convictions in the truth of the Bible strengthened my witness for Christ.

Do you see, dear friend, how beautiful the Lord has made you? He has bestowed on you the very beauty of the Lord Jesus Christ. He has done everything necessary to move you from the old life to make you completely brand-new. He has done for you what He did for His people in the Old Testament: claimed you as His own, covered your nakedness, washed you, wrapped you with fine linen, covered you with silk, adorned you with jewelry, placed a crown on your head, made you exceedingly beautiful, advanced you to royalty, and bestowed His very own splendor on you (Ezekiel 16:6-14). We know that we will be as "a bride adorned for her husband"; we will have "the glory of God" and "brilliance" like a costly stone (Revelation 21:2,10-11). We will see the face of our Lord, His name will be on our foreheads, He will give us light, and we will reign forever and ever (Revelation 22:3-5). Our only response is one of love, adoration, humility, and gratitude. More than that, because the Holy Spirit gives us this intimate relationship with Christ where we know Him, experience Him, and become like Him, we now draw near to Him and engage in a very real day-by-day, moment-by-moment communion and fellowship with our Lord.

In 1969, Charles Colson, a self-confessed political "kingmaker," was asked by President Nixon to join the circle of senior aides at the White House. Colson had made worldly success his entire goal in life. His desire for success was so great that he would do anything to attain it. At the White House, he became part of a group of brilliant men who shared two common threads: ego and ambition. Chuck Colson admits he was a master of manipulation. He sometimes sacrificed truth in the political arena and had the reputation of a cold-blooded political infighter. As he says of himself, he was willing at times to blink at certain ethical standards, to be ruthless when getting things done.

Before long, he found himself firmly enmeshed in a cover-up scandal that led to the first resignation of a United States president.

After leaving the White House, Colson met a business acquaintance named Tom Phillips, who, sensing a need in Colson, invited him into his home and told him bluntly about Jesus Christ. Phillips read from C.S. Lewis' *Mere Christianity.* Chuck Colson listened quietly, said goodnight, and left Phillips' home. But in the driveway, Colson found himself pierced to the heart by the words of Christ. He sobbed a prayer in a flood of tears, saying over and over, "Take me." After studying *Mere Christianity,* Chuck Colson determined to follow Jesus Christ for the rest of his life: "I don't just want to be saved. I don't just want to be forgiven. I want to be changed."

Well, indeed, he was transformed. He voluntarily pleaded guilty to a Watergate offense and was sent to prison for seven months, alongside "Mafia kingpins, drug dealers, and lifers." When he was released in January 1975, he found that God had planted a seed in his soul. He desired to bring real hope and inner change to those in prison. Passing up lucrative business opportunities, Colson founded Prison Fellowship, a ministry that introduces prisoners to Christ, disciples them, and equips them for transition to life outside the walls as contributing members of society. God has used Chuck Colson in a powerful way in the lives of thousands of prisoners, as well as the lives of thousands of volunteers who are a part of his ministry.

Oh, how incredible it is when God transforms a life. And that is what He will do in you as you are filled continually with the Holy Spirit. You will become a man or woman of God, fulfilling the plans and purposes He has in mind for you. He will set your heart on fire. And when your heart burns with love for Him, that love will spread to those around you.

My Response

DATE:

KEY VERSE: "But we all, with unveiled face, beholding as in a mirror the glory of the Lord, are being transformed into the same image from glory to glory, just as from the Lord, the Spirit" (2 Corinthians 3:18).

FOR FURTHER THOUGHT: How have you seen the transforming power of the Holy Spirit in your own life? Take some time now to thank the Lord for all He has done in you and for you.

MY RESPONSE:

HE GUIDES
YOUR STEPS

*Since we live by the Spirit, let us
keep in step with the Spirit.*

GALATIANS 5:25 NIV

The Holy Spirit is faithful to lead you if you are a child of God. "For all who are being led by the Spirit of God, these are sons of God" (Romans 8:14). Perhaps you have wondered what God's plan is for your life. Maybe you are weighing a decision that will alter the course of your life. Trust that the Holy Spirit will lead and guide you. The Greek word *ago* (translated "led") means "to guide, direct, and influence." The Lord will lead you just as He promised through Moses: "The LORD is the one who goes ahead of you; He will be with you. He will not fail you or forsake you. Do not fear or be dismayed" (Deuteronomy 31:8).

We see the leading of the Holy Spirit operative in the lives of the disciples in the early church in the book of Acts. The Spirit told Philip to go speak to the Ethiopian man in the chariot who was reading in the book of Isaiah (Acts 8:29). Philip explained the gospel, told him about Jesus, and the Ethiopian received Christ. The Spirit directed Peter to go to the house of Cornelius to explain the gospel (Acts 10:19), the Holy Spirit directed the early church to set apart Paul and Barnabas for a missionary journey, and the Spirit led Paul and Barnabas on that journey, beginning in Seleucia and continuing to Cyprus (Acts 13:2,4). They were forbidden by the Holy Spirit from going to Asia but instead were directed to Troas (Acts 16:6-8).

When you are filled with the Holy Spirit, you will receive guidance moment by moment, every day of your life. Paul encourages us with these words in Galatians: "So I say, let the Holy Spirit guide your lives... Since we are living by the Spirit, let us also follow the Spirit's leading in every part of our lives" (Galatians 5:16,25 NLT). Under the guidance of the Holy Spirit, the Lord will lead you on an incredibly exciting adventure. Following His guidance will require your faith, trust, and obedience as He leads you every step of the way.

J. Edwin Orr, possibly the greatest revivalist of all time, lived a spiritually exciting life because he was willing to trust in the Lord to lead him and provide for him. Orr recalls the remarkable stories of his early journeys with the Lord, his "apprenticeship of faith," in numerous taped sermons. Dr. Orr preached one of these sermons, "Personal Testimony and Repentance," more than 20 years ago at the Newport-Mesa Christian Center in Costa Mesa, California. His sermons have had such a profound impact on my own life that I would like to relate his personal testimony to you, as it excellently illustrates a Spirit-filled Christian's guidance by the Holy Spirit.

The Holy Spirit guided Orr to step out in faith in his ministry. "For we walk by faith, not by sight" (2 Corinthians 5:7). In the rural countryside of Ireland in the early 1900s, Orr was led to Christ by his mother when he was nine, but did not step out in faith to serve the Lord until he was 19. It went this way. Orr asked his friend Jim to go out preaching with him. Jim asked, "Can you preach?"

Orr replied, "No, can you?"

Jim said, "Well, I've read a paper from the Young People's Society."

Orr replied, "Well, I've read two papers!"

"Who is going to ask us to preach?" Jim asked.

Orr replied, "Why don't we start with open-air preaching? I'll invite you and you can invite me."

"I'm game if you're game, but how are we going to get a crowd?" Jim asked.

Orr answered, "We'll get a crowd all right."

Orr had a ukulele. His friend had a loud voice but could not sing a lick. Together, they drew a crowd of curious people. They preached only what they knew, which wasn't much at the time. But it was such a thrill for them, they decided to do it once a week. Soon they had 24 young men who preached with them in their open-air ministry.

The Holy Spirit guided Orr in his prayer life. "Pray without ceasing" (1 Thessalonians 5:17). One day Orr's group was talking about prayer. One of them asked, "Does God really answer prayer, or do things just happen?"

Orr suggested, "Let's keep a notebook of requests and see how God answers and keep track of those answers."

Their first prayer was for a louder instrument than a ukulele. Five days later they received a phone call from a guy who could play a banjo-mandolin. In 1932, they all attended an evangelistic meeting in Belfast, where the speaker talked about answered prayer. Orr pulled out their prayer notebook to see how many of their own prayers had been answered. He discovered that every prayer had been answered but one—the conversion of a man they all knew. Orr called the whole group together and said, "All our prayers have been answered but one." Then one of the young men came up to the group and said, "Did you hear, that man just got converted tonight!"

The Holy Spirit guided Orr in his vision for ministry. "Where there is no vision, the people perish" (Proverbs 29:18 KJV). Not long after that experience, the Lord gave Edwin Orr the idea to increase their little band of 24 men tenfold to 240. He asked his friend Jim what he thought about the idea. Jim answered that he would have to pray about it. A few days later, Jim came to Orr and related that he struggled with the idea but had gotten the victory, and he said he would join Orr in believing for 240 men in their group.

"You're too late," Orr responded. "God has increased my vision to 2400." And indeed, sooner than later, their group had grown to 2400 men.

The Holy Spirit guided Orr in trusting God to provide for him. "And my God will supply all your needs according to His riches in glory in Christ Jesus" (Philippians 4:19). A man from London contacted Orr and said he would pay him to evangelize all over the world. Orr was thrilled, made all the preparations, and quit his job. The day after he quit his job, the offer from London fell through. Orr still believed God was calling him to go to England and to begin a worldwide evangelistic ministry. This was during the Depression, and Orr was the sole provider for his mother and the rest of the family. His friends all thought he was crazy. He was 21 when he told his mother he was going to step out in faith. He promised that he would send her the same amount each week that he had been providing with his current job.

"Where will you get the money?" she asked.

"I don't know, but I'll send it," he answered.

A man paid Orr's way to Liverpool, England, in return for a favor. Orr arrived in Liverpool with 65 cents, a Bible, a change of clothes, and a bicycle. The only friend he had in Liverpool was an Irish scoutmaster he had met at a scout jamboree. Orr went to see him. His friend asked, "Where are you going to sleep at night?"

"In bed," Orr replied.

"Very funny. What about your next meal? Why don't you go to school for your vocation like most people?"

Orr replied, "But I'm called to be an evangelist."

"What does that mean?" the man queried.

Orr responded, "Well, an evangelist is one who travels with the gospel." The man offered to loan him some money if he would go back home to Ireland. But Orr assured him, "The Scripture says God will supply all my need."

The Holy Spirit guided Orr in opportunities for evangelism. "Live wisely among those who are not believers, and make the most of every opportunity" (Colossians 4:5 NLT). Orr began his journey there in Liverpool and rode his bicycle to Chester. Rain began to pour down on him, but he was able to ride about 40 miles beyond Chester to the little town of Shrewsbury, where he stopped in the pouring rain by the side of the road. A truck driver stopped across the street to tie a cover over some bags of sugar. The truck driver shouted across the road to Orr in a friendly way as if he knew him.

Orr knew he must have made a mistake. He wheeled his bicycle over and said, "Did you mistake me for someone?"

"I'm sorry," said the truck driver, "I thought you were a friend of mine, Bert Cook."

"That's funny, I have a friend called Bert Cook too."

"But you're not English," the man said.

"No, I'm from Ireland."

"I knew you were a foreigner the minute you opened your mouth. You wouldn't know the Bert Cook I know because he's English."

"I was in England once on a vacation at a place named Northampton, and the fellow I met was Herbert J. Cook, and he was studying to be a Methodist minister."

The truck driver looked at Orr in amazement and said, "Blimey, mate, it's the same bloke!" The population of England was 35 million, and this truck driver mistook Orr for one of the few Englishmen he knew. He said, "Where are you headed?"

"London," Orr replied, "but I won't go tonight—it would take me three days on a bicycle."

"How would you like to ride with me?"

"Are you going to London?" Orr asked.

The driver said, "No, I'm going the other way down toward Cardiff, but I'll take you as far as Wellington, about 10 miles east of Shrewsbury."

They tied the bicycle on the sugar bags, and Orr got in the comfortable cabin of the truck. They traveled on narrow winding roads with the rain falling hard. Orr began talking with the truck driver about Christ. His newfound friend was responsive. He said, "Well, Mr. Orr, if you're right, and I want to become a Christian, do I have to close my eyes when I pray?"

Orr smiled and said, "Brother, you can keep your eyes open while you're driving, and the Lord will understand." The truck driver was converted with his eyes open.

The Holy Spirit guided Orr into extraordinary experiences of God's power. "God's Spirit beckons. There are things to do and places to go" (Romans 8:14 MSG). Orr arrived at the next town and needed a place to stay. He had already spent some of his 65 cents and obviously was not going to be able to stay in the best hotel. He stopped to ask a policeman, "Can you tell me where I can get cheap accommodations for tonight?"

The policeman examined Orr suspiciously and asked, "What do you do for a living?" With so many transients looking for work, people in those days were often arrested for vagrancy.

What could Orr say—he wasn't a traveling bookkeeper, and he wasn't a traveling pastor, for he wasn't ordained. He replied, "I'm an evangelist."

"You don't look like an evangelist to me."

"What's an evangelist supposed to look like?" Orr asked.

"Well, you're very young," countered the policeman.

"No, I'm not. I'm 21."

"Well, that's very young for an evangelist. How long have you been an evangelist?"

Orr replied wryly, "Not very long."

"How long?" asked the policeman.

"Well, just a little while."

The policeman said, "I have reasons for asking. How long have you been an evangelist?"

"Sir, if you insist on being technical, I started at eight o'clock this morning."

The policeman asked, "Do you have anything to show me that you're genuine?"

"Well, I have some letters of introduction."

The policeman said, "Show me one."

Orr thought, *Which one should I show him?* He had a letter written by an Episcopal rector to show people in the church of England, a letter written by a Presbyterian minister to show to people at the church of Scotland, letters written by Methodist, Baptist, Plymouth, and Pentecostal ministers, and then a letter by an obscure friend, not well-known, who worked in a little storefront mission. The last was the most enthusiastic, so Orr decided to show it to him.

The policeman read it very thoroughly and then warmly shook hands with Orr. He was a converted policeman, a deacon in the local Baptist church, and a close friend of William Phillip, who had written the letter. The policeman had just seen him the previous week and had met him at Wales at a convention. The policeman took Orr home, and that night Orr slept in a feather bed. The next morning he ate two eggs for breakfast. That is how he began to see that God would lead, guide, and provide for him. He realized that if God could take care of him today, He could take care of him tomorrow, next month, and next year. Orr lived a life of faith like that his entire life until he stepped from time into eternity in 1987.

Why do I share with you the story of Orr's leading by the Holy Spirit? You and I need to remember that as the Holy Spirit led the Old Testament servants of God, as He led Jesus, as He led the disciples of the first-century church, as He led such men and women of God as J. Edwin Orr and Amy Carmichael, so He will lead and guide you. What is your response? How can you set your sail to catch the guiding wind of the Holy Spirit? Will you believe God for the great adventure He has prepared just for you? Will you believe God for God-sized activity? Then, dear friend, be filled with the Spirit, set your sail, and enter into the adventure.

My Response

DATE:

KEY VERSE: Paul said, "For all who are being led by the Spirit of God, these are sons of God" (Romans 8:14).

FOR FURTHER THOUGHT: Have you entered into the great adventure of knowing God and being led by Him in your life? Will you step over the line of self-sufficiency and look for God to lead you and guide you in life? Write a prayer to the Lord, expressing all that is on your heart.

MY RESPONSE:

HE BRINGS UNITY
TO THE CHURCH

*[Be] diligent to preserve the unity of the
Spirit in the bond of peace. There is one
body and one Spirit, just as also you were
called in one hope of your calling.*

EPHESIANS 4:3-4

T he Holy Spirit brings unity and community to the church of Jesus
Christ. Paul instructs us to be "diligent to preserve the unity of
the Spirit in the bond of peace. There is one body and one Spirit, just
as also you were called in one hope of your calling" (Ephesians 4:3-4).
Even though the church is a body with many members, the Holy Spirit
gives us unity in the body of believers. The Greek word *henotes* (translated "unity") means "oneness without division." We are to move with
fluidity and harmony as the body, with Christ, the head, controlling and
empowering us through His Spirit. Only then will the fruit of the Holy
Spirit be manifest in the body of the church as believers are continually
filled with the Spirit.

The church is also like a building put together by the Holy Spirit.

This is a picture of the structural sense of community. The church is "God's household, having been built on the foundation of the apostles and prophets, Christ Jesus Himself being the corner stone, in whom the whole building, being fitted together, is growing into a holy temple in the Lord, in whom you also are being built together into a dwelling of God in the Spirit" (Ephesians 2:19-22). You are never alone in this world. You are an integral part of the body of Christ and are structurally being fitted together with others in the church into a holy community, a holy dwelling place for God Himself.

What will happen in the church as a community when the Holy Spirit is at work? The church will enjoy unity as the Holy Spirit guides and empowers the church's worship, teaching, fellowship, ministry, and evangelism.

Worship. The Holy Spirit not only inspires us to worship, He teaches those in the church how to worship. Jesus said, "But an hour is coming, and now is, when the true worshipers will worship the Father in spirit and truth; for such people the Father seeks to be His worshipers" (John 4:23). The Greek word *proskuneo* (translated "worship") means "to adore, revere, and do homage" to the Lord. Worship is a corporate expression of our love, awe, and devotion to our Lord. These expressions may include music, prayer, and even silence.

R.C. Sproul says that forms, structures, and liturgy in our corporate worship can "be a means of grace if grounded in the Word and practiced from the heart."[1] We know that the Holy Spirit helps us in prayer and "testifies with our spirit that we are children of God" (Romans 8:16,26). His work in us turns our hearts to love and thankfulness, expressing itself in delight and reverence. Heaven is filled with worship (Revelation 4–5) and so should be the church.

Teaching. The Holy Spirit encourages us to grow spiritually, teaching us through the Word of God. We are to "grow up in all aspects into Him who is the head, even Christ" (Ephesians 4:15). J.I. Packer speaks of the importance of learning among Christians: "One great need today is a renewal of systematic Christian instruction."[2] Our instruction should begin with the Bible as our textbook because it is "inspired by God and is useful to teach us what is true and to make us realize what is wrong in our lives. It corrects us when we are wrong and teaches us to do what is right. God uses it to prepare and equip his people to do every good work" (2 Timothy 3:16-17 NLT). God has given the church those who have the gift of teaching to help others learn and grow (1 Corinthians 12:28).

Fellowship. "The grace of the Lord Jesus Christ, and the love of God, and the fellowship of the Holy Spirit, be with you all" (2 Corinthians 13:14). The Greek word *koinonia* ("fellowship") points to participation that comes from the Holy Spirit. Fellowship is an intimate sharing with one another, a sense of oneness with purpose, a sense of community. Perhaps this account of the early church in Acts describes it best:

> And all those who had believed were together and had all things in common; and they began selling their property and possessions and were sharing them with all, as anyone might have need. Day by day continuing with one mind in the temple, and breaking bread from house to house, they were taking their meals together with gladness and sincerity of heart, praising God and having favor with all the people. And the Lord was adding to their number day by day those who were being saved (Acts 2:44-47).

When I was in college and serving with Campus Crusade for Christ, I frequently invited my friends over to my house for times of fellowship. Sometimes, a few dozen young people would cram into our living room. We shared together what God was teaching us, a verse from the Bible, or a prayer request. Then we would all pray together. These were cherished times of community to me and to us all. Community occurs when a group of individual believers will communicate honestly, remove the masks to vulnerability, challenge each other to higher spiritual ground, exhort each other with the Word of God, pray for one another, and share in common joys, delights, suffering, and sorrows.

Ministry. The Holy Spirit equips believers to carry out their ministry. "But to each one is given a manifestation of the Spirit for the common good" (1 Corinthians 12:7). The Greek word *sumphero* ("common good") means "to bring together, profit, contribute, and benefit the common purpose." Ministry is designed by God to positively benefit the church.

Ken Horton, a pastor in Fort Worth, Texas, shares the joy of ministry: "One of the greatest sources of satisfaction is seeing people you've worked with move on to develop their own ministries. We encourage our leaders to make this their goal—to find their own spiritual fulfillment by seeing others develop a joyful, fruitful ministry."[3] The Greek word *diakonia* ("ministry") describes service in the Christian community. This service occurs in the church, both locally and universally, with varieties of effects determined by God.

Evangelism. Jesus has given us the Great Commission: "Go therefore and make disciples of all the nations, baptizing them in the name of the Father and the Son and the Holy Spirit, teaching them to observe all that I commanded you; and lo, I am with you always, even to the end of the age" (Matthew 28:19-20). What is Jesus' plan of evangelism? It is a simple plan of multiplication by discipleship. Men and women are won to Christ, built up in their Christian faith, and sent out to tell others about Christ.

The one who fuels the fire of discipleship and evangelism is the Holy Spirit. Jesus said, "But you will receive power when the Holy Spirit has come upon you; and you shall be My witnesses both in Jerusalem, and in all Judea and Samaria, and even to the remotest part of the earth" (Acts 1:8). In fact, nothing of evangelism is done without the Holy Spirit. Dr. Bill Bright speaks of the extraordinary results of being filled with the Holy Spirit, "Today, if enough Christians were completely committed to our resurrected and returning Lord and were controlled and empowered by His Spirit, we would turn our world upside down and experience a spiritual revolution like that first century revolution."[4] God has said, "Not by might nor by power, but by My Spirit" (Zechariah 4:6).

Unity is imperative for the church body to function properly because "we are members of His body" (Ephesians 5:30). Every member is important. Think about the human body. Every part of your human body is important if you are to function properly. The church needs every believer to exercise his or her spiritual gifts if the church body is to function the way Christ intended. To that end, the church is to be pure and holy. "Christ also loved the church and gave Himself up for her, so that He might sanctify her, having cleansed her by the washing of water with the word, that He might present to Himself the church in all her glory, having no spot or wrinkle or any such thing; but that she would be holy and blameless" (Ephesians 5:25-27). The Holy Spirit has a message for the church today, and it is found in the letters to the churches in Revelation 2–3. One phrase is repeated over and over again: "He who has an ear, let him hear what the Spirit says to the churches" (Revelation 2:7,11,17,29; 3:6,13,22).

Let's explore the two principle dangers facing the church today, revealed in Jesus' letters to the churches in Revelation 2–3: compromise and complacency.

Compromise involves unholy alliances and affections. Jesus told the church at Ephesus, "You have left your first love" (Revelation 2:4). He didn't say they had lost their love, but they had walked away from their love for Him. What will threaten your love for Jesus Christ? Unholy alliances and affections. Do you love anything more than Christ? Have you ever loved Christ more than you do now? Do you talk with Him, listen to what He says in His Word, and commune with Him? The Holy Spirit will sift your priorities and affections, casting light on those unholy alliances. His fire is a purifying fire, taking out the impurities and making you like pure gold (James 1:3; 1 Peter 1:7).

Charles Trumbull warns, "Danger lies ahead when we begin to tolerate breaks and failures as the expected rather than the unexpected, the usual instead of the unusual, and it becomes habitual."[5] There comes a day, dear friend, when you must make a dramatic move, put away those childish things, and become a mature man or woman of conviction. It is imperative that the church "learn what is pleasing to the Lord" (Ephesians 5:10).

What is the answer if you have left your first love? Repentance. Change and return to your love for Christ. Dear friend, repentance is possible only through the power of the Holy Spirit in you. Run to the Lord, confess your sin, and ask Him to fill you with His Holy Spirit. Surrender to God, and He will fill you with a new passion for Christ. He will do for you what you cannot do for yourself, and your love for Christ will grow more and more.

Always remember Paul's words to the Galatians: "After starting your Christian lives in the Spirit, why are you now trying to become perfect by your own human effort?" (Galatians 3:3 NLT). When you give yourself to

God, you will express your love to Him anew. The Holy Spirit will work in you to help you say no to unholy alliances and affections.

Sometimes that no will be drastic and dramatic, such as when Joseph had to run out of Potiphar's house (Genesis 39:6-18). That is why Paul says, "But the one who joins himself to the Lord is one spirit with Him. Flee immorality…Or do you not know that your body is a temple of the Holy Spirit who is in you, whom you have from God, and that you are not your own? For you have been bought with a price: therefore glorify God in your body" (1 Corinthians 6:17-20). James tells us that God "jealously yearns for the Spirit that He causes to dwell in your hearts" (James 4:5 Williams). He encourages us to "submit to God. Resist the devil and he will fly from you. Draw near to God and He will draw near to you…Humble yourselves before the Lord, and He will lift you high" (verses 7-10). Always remember you are the bride of Christ. Make it your ambition to be faithful to your Bridegroom.

Complacency, the second danger facing the church today, means you are lukewarm rather than on fire in your devotion to Christ. Jesus said to the church at Laodicea, "I know your deeds, that you are neither cold nor hot; I wish that you were cold or hot. So because you are lukewarm, and neither hot nor cold, I will spit you out of My mouth" (Revelation 3:15-16). The Lord Jesus knows you and sees all the way into your heart. He knows exactly where you are with Him. How's your heart these days? Is your heart on fire for Jesus Christ? If not, do you know what the answer is? Again, the key is to repent, to change your mind for the better.

How can you become hot with a heart on fire for Christ? Jesus rebukes the church at Laodicea: "Therefore, shake off your complacency and repent. See, I stand knocking at the door. If anyone listens to my voice and opens the door, I will go into his house, and dine with him, and he with me" (Revelation 3:19-20 Phillips). Dear friend, the greatest answer for a lukewarm heart is to lay aside every other thing, grab hold of your Bible, and spend some good, uninterrupted time with your Lord. He is waiting for you. Will you draw near to Him? The promise from James 4:8 holds true for you: "Draw near to God and He will draw near to you." God offered a similar promise to Judah when the nation was going into exile: "You will seek Me and find Me when you search for Me with all your heart" (Jeremiah 29:13).

One of the greatest reasons people drift away from God and live with compromise and complacency is that they lack aim or direction. Lot is the perfect example of a life with no goals. He chose the things of the world and lost everyone and everything dear to Him. Abraham, his uncle, chose the things of God and followed the ways of the Lord. He built altars and worshipped God all along the way on his journey. Abraham enjoyed such an intimate friendship with the Lord that He "remained with Abraham" a little longer just to converse with him (Genesis 18:22 NLT). The Lord singled Abraham out, blessed him, and fulfilled His promises to him (verses 17-19).

Paul encourages believers to "run to win! All athletes are disciplined in their training. They do it to win a prize that will fade away, but we do it for an eternal prize. So I run with purpose in every step" (1 Corinthians 9:24-26 NLT). One of disciplines that helps me run my race with purpose and keeps me from drifting is to set spiritual goals every year. I like to sit down with the Lord and think about what direction I'm working toward spiritually and what I'd like to do in ministry. Sometimes people ask me how I do so many things in ministry. Writing out spiritual goals is the secret.

For many years now, I have made a practice of going on a yearly mini-retreat, stepping away from the demands of life and drawing near to the Lord for guidance and direction. I choose what I would like to study in the Bible for the year, what Bible reading plan I will use, which books I would like to read, which devotional books I will use in my quiet time, when I will have my quiet time, and what I'd like to accomplish in ministry. I've included a spiritual goals worksheet in the appendix 4 to help you set some spiritual goals so you can be like Paul and run with purpose in every step.

Christ loves the church. He nourishes and cherishes it, and we should also. I love the church, and I am passionate about seeing the church love and serve God as the body of Christ. I live and breathe to see those in the church come to know and love the Lord and bring Him glory. I am absolutely committed to seeing men and women take Bibles off shelves and open them day by day, live in them, and draw near to God. I am so thankful for those who have gone before us, such as Charles Spurgeon, D.L. Moody, A.W. Tozer, J. Edwin Orr, Amy Carmichael, Corrie ten

Boom, and so many others who have faithfully served in the body of Christ. May we who follow in their train be found faithful in contributing with our gifts and service to the ministry of the church. We will know it was worth it all when we hear the words of our Lord, "Well done, good and faithful servant."

My Response

DATE:

KEY VERSE: "[Be] diligent to preserve the unity of the Spirit in the bond of peace. There is one body and one Spirit, just as also you were called in one hope of your calling" (Ephesians 4:3-4).

FOR FURTHER THOUGHT: What was the most important truth you learned about the church today? Did the Holy Spirit convict you of anything you need to change in order to love and serve the Lord in the church? Will you set aside time for a mini-retreat to draw near to the Lord and think through spiritual goals for your life? You may choose to use the spiritual goals worksheet in appendix 4.

MY RESPONSE:

Day Twenty-Eight

HE IGNITES
CORPORATE
REVIVALS

"Son of man, can these bones live?"…
Thus says the Lord GOD to these bones,
"Behold, I will cause breath to enter
you that you may come to life."

EZEKIEL 37:3-5

The Holy Spirit ignites widespread corporate revivals in His own time and in His own way. Perhaps God is preparing to pour out His Spirit in a powerful way in our present generation. God gave the prophet Ezekiel a picture of how He works in revival by taking him in a vision to a valley of dry bones (Ezekiel 37). Ezekiel describes his experience: "The hand of the LORD was upon me, and He brought me out by the Spirit of the LORD and set me down in the middle of the valley; and it was full of bones." These bones were not just dry, but "very dry." And many bones were on the surface of the valley.

Is this not like our world today? Many dry, lifeless people around the world race through a temporal existence that will soon pass away. The entertainment world would have you desire a lifestyle that is not life at all, but merely dry bones. God gives the true picture of so many in a world going nowhere.

God asked Ezekiel, "Son of man, can these bones live?" And God did indeed bring those bones to life: "The breath came into them, and they came to life and stood on their feet, an exceedingly great army." Of course, God gave this vision to Ezekiel to encourage His people that they were never without hope. God would indeed bring them back to life, even in the desperation of their exile. But He interprets this picture of giving life to dry bones further for us: " 'I will put My Spirit within you and you will come to life, and I will place you on your own land. Then you will know that I, the LORD, have spoken and done it,' declares the LORD." Imagine the Holy Spirit bringing a whole valley of dry bones to life and building a great army in the process.

And so it is that the breath of God, the Holy Spirit, fills whole groups of men and women and brings them to life. We know that Jesus breathed on His entire group of disciples and said to them, "Receive the Holy Spirit" (John 20:22). We know that Scripture was God-breathed and that the Word of God is living and active. Oh how mighty and powerful is the breath of God. And when God breathes over large groups of people, pouring out His Spirit in powerful ways, we experience a corporate revival.

The breath of corporate revival swept over the Scottish Isle of Lewis in 1949. The story is told of two elderly women, both in their eighties and one blind, who suddenly became greatly burdened because of the appalling spiritual state of their own parish. Not a single young person attended church or public worship. Where were the young Christian leaders of the future? These two women were so concerned that they began specifically praying for God to work in their church. Gripped by Isaiah 44:3—"For I will pour water on the thirsty land and streams upon the dry ground"—they prayed for God to do something powerful. They frequently got on their knees at ten in the evening, and remained on their knees in prayer until three or four in the morning.

One of the ministers of the parish came to visit these women at their home. The women suggested they move the prayer meeting to a nearby barn. The minister called his elders together, and seven of them met in a barn to pray on Tuesday and Friday. One night, as the elders and the two women were kneeling there in the barn and praying, a young deacon got up and read Psalm 24:3-5 (KJV): "Who shall ascend into the hill of the LORD? Or who shall stand in his holy place? He that hath clean hands, and a pure heart; who hath not lifted up his soul unto vanity, nor sworn deceitfully. He shall receive the blessing from the LORD." And then that young man closed his Bible. Looking down at the minister and the elders, he said that all their prayers were wasted if they all were not willing to be holy and pure themselves. Then he lifted his two hands and prayed, "God, are my hands clean? Is my heart pure?" But he got no further.

At that moment he and the other ministers were gripped by the conviction that revival must be related to holiness and godliness. When that conviction of holiness came to those in the barn, the power of God swept through those in attendance and on into the parish. And an awareness of God—true revival—gripped the community such as hadn't been known for more than a hundred years. The following day, the looms were silent, and little work was done on the farms as men and women gave themselves to thinking on eternal things, gripped by eternal truths.

In those first days of the Lewis revival in 1949, the congregation would leave the church, ready to go home. And then, moved by the irresistible power of the Holy Spirit, they would go back into the church, and a wave of conviction would sweep over the gathering, moving strong men to cry out to God for mercy. So great was the distress and deep the hunger for God that they refused to go home. Within a matter of days, spiritual awakening had gripped churches everywhere in the area, with services continuing until three in the morning. Both young and old put work aside and came face-to-face with eternal realities.

Indifference to the things of God had been great in the town of Arnol. A wave of revival swept the village, and some said that while one man prayed, the very house shook. The tavern in one village was put out of business because the men who frequented it were now in prayer meetings. One young man, speaking for many of the youth in one area, said, "We did not know what church going meant until the revival came; now the prayer meeting is the weekly attraction, and the worship of God in His house on the Sabbath our chief delight."

I confess I haven't had the great opportunity to witness the power of corporate revival like that on the Isle of Lewis in 1949. But I did experience an unexpected, powerful move of the Holy Spirit at a church retreat a number of years ago. The group of women I was speaking to was sharing the dining room with another group of women from a nearby town. I was scheduled to speak in the afternoon. As we all sat there together, suddenly the thought came to me, *What if we all sang and worshipped God together?*

It was just a thought, but someone started singing. Then others joined in. The presence of God fell on us through the power of the Holy Spirit in a way that I had never experienced before. I can only describe His presence as pure love. We were all standing and singing together, two groups in the common bond of Christ, one song after another, in perfect harmony. No one wanted to leave. This worship continued for more than two hours, well past the time I was to speak. I have never forgotten this amazing experience, and I believe the Lord allowed me to have just a glimpse of what those days of corporate revival are really like when the Holy Spirit falls upon a large group of believers.

I want you to know something very personal. I am believing God for corporate revival in the church throughout the world. And I am praying that He will breathe the wind of the Holy Spirit through our lands in the valleys of dry bones and bring about widespread revival, causing those dry bones to come to life. History has recorded many powerful revivals, including the Welsh revival of 1904–1905, the Great Awakening, and the Second Great Awakening. Oh, how I pray God will send us another. Will you join with me in praying for revival? J. Edwin Orr, our Irish revivalist friend of the early 1900s, was asked what someone could do to help bring about revival. Orr responded, "Let it begin with you." May it be so with us.

My Response

DATE:

KEY VERSE: "'Son of man, can these bones live?'...Thus says the Lord God to these bones, 'Behold, I will cause breath to enter you that you may come to life'" (Ezekiel 37:3-5).

FOR FURTHER THOUGHT: Describe in your own words what corporate revival looks like. Will you pray for revival in your church and in your land? And dear friend, will you let that revival begin with you?

MY RESPONSE:

Day Twenty-Nine

BECOMING AN INSTRUMENT OF REVIVAL

But we have this treasure in earthen vessels,
so that the surpassing greatness of the power
will be of God and not from ourselves.

2 CORINTHIANS 4:7

God desires for you to experience personal revival and perhaps even to be an instrument of corporate revival. God has always had the intention of doing God-sized works through willing men and women. Paul knew God's power was at work in his ministry: "But we have this treasure in earthen vessels, so that the surpassing greatness of the power will be of God and not from ourselves" (2 Corinthians 4:7). Henrietta Mears always said to dream big because anything less than a big vision is unworthy of our great God. The Lord delights in taking nobodies who will talk about Somebody—the one and only, Jesus—with anybody.

In your earthen vessel, you will face the same trials Paul and other disciples faced: affliction, perplexity, persecution, setbacks, and outward decay. But because of the Holy Spirit in you, you have something the rest of the world does not have—hope. Paul tied this hope to the power of the Holy Spirit: "Now may the God of hope fill you with all joy and peace in believing, so that you will abound in hope by the power of the Holy Spirit" (Romans 15:13). Where others give up, you will not. You may be down, but you are never out. Others may say it's over for you. But according to God's Word, you are exactly where God wants you because in the midst of your trials, He can do mighty works. You need to pray for the faith of Abraham, a "hope against hope" kind of faith that sees the invisible, holds on to the promises of God, and watches eagerly to see what God is going to do. That's the kind of person God can use.

Who is the person God uses? One who is Holy Spirit–driven and Holy Spirit–led and Holy Spirit–filled. Oh, look out when the Holy Spirit is at work. The person God uses listens to the voice of the Lord in His Word, not the voice of the world. The person God uses takes the path less traveled and makes the sacred climb to know God. The person God uses sees all of life from an eternal perspective and breathes air that is clean and pure in the presence of God.

But you pay a price when you are used by God, dear friend. You no longer belong to yourself but to God. Lay aside every encumbrance and the sin that so easily entangles you (Hebrews 12:1-2). If you are not right with God, get right with God and pray to be filled with the Holy Spirit. When you stand at the crossroads, take the right road, go into training with the Holy Spirit as your trainer and coach, and take on the study of God's Word. Ask your Lord to teach you to pray. Then begin the climb to know and love God with all your heart, soul, mind, and strength. Ask Him to set your heart on fire. Then watch expectantly. He will use you in more ways than you can imagine, and you will be one of His instruments to revive those around you, drawing others to Himself.

When you are led into a closer walk with God and a deeper understanding of God, He is getting you to a place where He can set your heart on fire for Him. When the Holy Spirit comes and fills you, you are saturated with the presence of God, and your heart begins to burn on fire for Christ. Personal revival has begun. The presence of God shines from you as from a light on a hill. There is no mistaking a heart on fire for Christ. When you burn for Christ, you stand apart from the tinsel and glitter of the world. When others see the light of the fire of Christ, they are drawn to Him.

I wonder if you would be willing to say yes to the commitment of a burning heart, a heart in love with Jesus Christ and on fire for Him. If you are willing to say yes to the Lord, join me in a new fellowship, the Fellowship of Hearts on Fire. Your commitment to a heart on fire is a purposeful yielding of yourself to your Lord and includes quiet time, living by God's Word, holy living, sharing Christ with others in His power, and abandonment to the will of God as His disciple. It is a radical commitment to intimacy with God, the authority of God's Word, personal revival, the power of the Holy Spirit, and discipleship by Christ Himself. You make this commitment out of love for Him because you belong to God through faith in Christ.

Are you willing to be led and taught by your Lord through the ongoing work of the Holy Spirit in you? You and I will still sin and go the wrong way at times. But our Lord is faithful to show us our sin, and He will lead and guide us in life. Ruth Paxson says, "It is not *in order to be His,* but *because we are His* that we yield our lives to Him. Purchase gives title to property, but it is only delivery that gives possession."[1] The commitment to a heart on fire is the resolve that the Lord will have possession of what He gave His life for: you and me.

I invite you to turn to appendix 5 and read and study the commitments of the Fellowship of Hearts on Fire. Dear friend, I invite you to sign these commitments as a testimony to the fire the Lord is causing to burn in your heart. Together, through the power of the Holy Spirit, we will be part of this fellowship. I cannot wait to see what God is going to accomplish through our lives.

> Revival commences with those who in bad times remain good, in godless days remain Christian, in careless years remain constant and who have eternity in their hearts. Revival begins with those who stand firm, like Hezekiah, in an age of godless rejection, in an age when the people do what is right in their own eyes. It begins with the man who stands for that which is true and right and good; but it also requires a man who can see what the state of the church and the nation really is.[2]

Only the Holy Spirit can produce such men and women who will rise up to the great call of God in Jesus Christ. May we be those men and women of God who are members of another kingdom, the kingdom of God, and who live out our brief stay on earth as instruments of revival, earthen vessels filled with the power of the Holy Spirit and with hearts set on fire for Jesus Christ.

My Response

DATE:

KEY VERSE: "But we have this treasure in earthen vessels, so that the surpassing greatness of the power will be of God and not from ourselves" (2 Corinthians 4:7).

FOR FURTHER THOUGHT: In what ways has the Lord set your own heart on fire? How will you apply what you have learned on this 30-day journey? What is the most important truth you have learned? What commitments to Christ have you made as a result of this time in God's Word? Prayerfully spend time reading through and considering the commitments of the Fellowship of Hearts on Fire in appendix 5. Find out more about this fellowship at www.setmyheartonfire.com.

MY RESPONSE:

QUIET TIME
WEEK FIVE:
LET THE RIVERS
OF LIVING
WATER FLOW

If anyone is thirsty, let him come to Me
and drink. He who believes in Me, as
the Scripture said, From his innermost
being will flow rivers of living water.
But this He spoke of the Spirit.

JOHN 7:37-39

PREPARE YOUR HEART

One spark can ignite the fire of a revival. Sometimes only God knows what the spark is, only He sees the ignition of revival fire, and the people are left to experience the effects of it. In the case of the Welsh Revival of 1904–1905, the spark is known, and the instrument of revival was Evan Roberts. He was a young man who had been praying for revival since the age of 13. His heart caught fire when he was willing to take the Word of God into his own heart and get personal with God. He heard a preacher cry out, "Lord, bend us!" That prayer was not good enough for Evan Roberts. He was compelled to run to the front of the room and cry out, "Lord, bend me!" He said that when he prayed that prayer for himself, his heart was ablaze with the desire to go the length and breadth of Wales to tell others about Christ. He became the instrument of God in a great revival where the entire country was like a great prayer meeting. When the fire of God falls on hearts through the Holy Spirit, no one can stop the blaze that erupts. Oh, that God will do it again.

Begin your time with the Lord by asking Him to cause your heart to catch fire and to let rivers of living water flow with incredible power from your life.

READ AND STUDY GOD'S WORD

1. Read John 7:37-39. What is Jesus' promise in these words?

2. What can create thirst in the hearts of men and women?

3. In what way would Jesus' promise in John 7:37-39 answer the thirst of men and women?

ADORE GOD IN PRAYER

Take time now to ask the Lord to continually set your heart on fire and cause the rivers of living water to flow in and through you.

YIELD YOURSELF TO GOD

Close by meditating on these words by Mrs. Charles Cowman:

I saw a human life ablaze with God,
I felt a power divine
As through an empty vessel of frail clay
I saw God's glory shine.

Then woke I from a dream, and cried aloud:
My Father, give to me
The blessing of a life consumed by God
That I may live for Thee.[1]

Enjoy His Presence

Turn back to day 1 and read what you wrote in your letter to the Lord. As you think about experiencing the power of the Holy Spirit in this 30-day journey, summarize in a few sentences the most important truths you have learned. How will this journey make a difference in your life, and what will you carry with you?

Rest in His Love

"And the Lord will continually guide you, and satisfy your desire in scorched places, and give strength to your bones; and you will be like a watered garden, and like a spring of water whose waters do not fail" (Isaiah 58:11).

Notes — Week Five

APPENDIXES

DISCUSSION QUESTIONS

≫

These questions are for people who share this 30-day journey together. This book is a great tool for talking together about the person and ministry of the Holy Spirit. It also provides for a great 30-day preparation for one of the books of quiet times available from Quiet Time Ministries. God bless you as you help others embrace the Holy Spirit and His work in their lives.

Introduction

Use the introduction week to meet those in your group, hand out copies of this book, familiarize everyone with the topic of the Holy Spirit, and play the introduction message (if you are using the weekly DVD messages for *Set My Heart on Fire*). Begin your group time by asking, "What brought you to this 30-day journey? How did you hear about it?" Allow everyone to share. Then pass out the books and show those in your group how each week is organized, with a quiet time as the sixth day. Show your group all the appendixes. Tell them about the websites www.setmyheartonfire.com, www.quiettime.org, and www.myquiettime.com and about the Quiet Time Café message board at www.quiettimecafe.com, where they may share insights online with others. Then describe how each week you will structure your weekly meetings. You may want to use a signup sheet for snacks. Close in prayer.

Week One: God Has a Plan for You
DAY 1—On the Emmaus Road

1. Begin your time together in prayer. You may want to open your time of discussion by reading the poem by Annie Johnson Flint at the end of day 5.

2. Have someone read the verse at the beginning of each day. Ask your group to share what it meant to them to spend daily time this last week thinking about the power of the Holy Spirit.

3. Why is the Holy Spirit important in our lives?

4. Describe the event on the road to Emmaus. What happened in the lives of those two men that changed them?

5. What was your favorite statement in day 1 about the Emmaus Road? What challenged you? What encouraged you?

6. If you prayed the prayer to receive Christ for the first time, you can know that the Lord Jesus lives in you and that you are born again to a living hope (1 Peter 1:3).

DAY 2—When Your Heart Catches Fire

1. In day 2 you saw that when your heart catches fire, you experience power in your life. Jesus promised power to His disciples in Acts 1:8. What was He promising to give His disciples?

2. How did you see His promise lived out in the disciples' lives?

3. What did you learn about weakness?

4. How was Paul an example of power perfected in weakness? How was Charles Spurgeon an example of power perfected in weakness?

5. What was your favorite insight from day 2?

Day 3—Run Before the Wind

1. What does being filled with the Holy Spirit mean?

2. What must we do in order to be filled with the Holy Spirit?

3. What does the metaphor of running before the wind mean, and why is this a good example of being filled with the Holy Spirit?

4. Which of these do you find most challenging in your own life: confession, surrender, prayer, or following the leading of God? Why?

5. What happens when you are filled with the Holy Spirit?

Day 4—Setting Your Sail

1. What does the metaphor of setting your sail to catch the wind of the Holy Spirit mean to you?

2. What are ways you can set your sail to catch the wind of the Holy Spirit in your life?

3. What is the difference between a fleshly Christian and a spiritual Christian?

4. What is the secret of displaying the fruit of the Holy Spirit and living like a spiritual Christian instead of a fleshly Christian?

Day 5—At the Crossroads

1. Why is it important to stop and look at who you are and where you are going in life?

2. As you thought through some of the very searching questions in this day's reading, what convicted you the most? Where could you see that you have experienced spiritual growth?

3. As you think through these deep spiritual truths, what do you think is most important for the church today?

4. What was your favorite quote from the reading in day 5?

DAY 6—Quiet Time Week One: A Heart on Fire for Christ

1. On day 6 your quiet time focused on having a heart on fire for Christ. What is a heart on fire? Describe someone who has a heart on fire.

2. What difference can a heart on fire for Christ make in the world?

3. Have you known someone who has such a heart? How has that person's life made a difference in your life?

4. What quote, verse, or insight encouraged you the most this week?

Week Two: The Person of the Holy Spirit
DAY 7—He Is Your God

1. Quickly review what you discussed last week. This will be of special benefit to those who are just joining your group. You might review by sharing what it means to be filled with the Holy Spirit. Then share the illustration of running before the wind and the great need for us to set our sail to catch the wind of the Holy Spirit. You might share how God's power is perfected in weakness and that your weakness actually qualifies you for service. As you lead your group through a discussion of each day in week 2, you may want to have someone read the verse at the beginning of each day.

2. In day 7 we looked at the Holy Spirit as the third person of the triune God. Ask your group what they learned about the Holy Spirit's divinity: His divine Person, His attributes, and His personality. What do we learn in the Word of God that demonstrates the Holy Spirit is the third person of the triune God?

3. What did you learn about the Holy Spirit that was new to you?

4. What was your favorite truth about the Holy Spirit in today's reading?

DAY 8—He Is Your Salvation

1. On day 8 you learned that the Holy Spirit is intimately involved in your salvation. What is the Holy Spirit's role in your salvation?

2. How do salvation and the work of the Holy Spirit make a difference in a person's life?

3. How was Paul an example of this dynamic life change? How did Charles Finney's life demonstrate the saving work of the Holy Spirit?

4. How has your life changed as a result of experiencing salvation and trusting Christ as your Savior and Lord?

DAY 9—He Is Your Comforter

1. In day 9 you learned that the Holy Spirit is your Comforter. What does that mean? What does He do in your life?

2. Why did Jesus pray for another Comforter in your life? What did He desire for you in your life?

3. In what ways do you need the Comforter, the Helper, in your life today?

DAY 10—He Is Your Indwelling Glory

1. In day 10 you learned that the Lord now lives in you through the indwelling Holy Spirit. How did looking at the Old Testament tabernacle help you better understand the presence of God in your own life?

2. What does being a temple of the Holy Spirit mean to you? How does knowing this make a difference in the way you live?

3. A threefold response to the presence of God in you spells HIM. What do those letters stand for, and which one meant the most to you in this last week in relation to God's presence in you?

Day 11—He Is Your Guarantee of Eternal Life

1. In day 11 you learned that you were sealed in Christ by the Holy Spirit and were given the Holy Spirit as a pledge. What does this mean, and why are these truths so important?

2. How does the promise of heaven change the way you live today?

Day 12—Quiet Time Week Two: The Magnificent Holy Spirit

1. In your quiet time this week, you had the opportunity to look at different verses about the Holy Spirit. What was the most significant truth you learned about the Holy Spirit from these verses?

2. From everything you have studied this week, summarize why you need the Holy Spirit.

3. How did this week of reading influence your thinking and understanding about the Holy Spirit in your life?

4. What was your favorite insight, quote, or verse from your reading and study this week? What have you thought about most this week as you have engaged in this 30-day journey?

Week Three: The Presence of the Holy Spirit
Day 13—He Makes Christ Known to You

1. In the last two weeks we have been talking about who the Holy Spirit is and why we need Him in our lives. We have seen that those who live in the power of the Holy Spirit act differently from those who don't. What is the most important thing you've learned so far in this 30-day journey about the power of the Holy Spirit? (As you lead your group through a discussion of each day in week 3, you may want to have someone read the verse at the beginning of each day.)

2. In day 13 you learned that the Holy Spirit enables you to experience the presence of Christ. How does experiencing the presence of Christ relate to having a heart that burns on fire for the Lord?

3. What will you experience as a result of Christ living in you? What is the outward evidence of Christ in you?

4. What meant the most to you in the examples in day 13 of those who love Christ?

Day 14—He Fills You with Love

1. In day 14 we looked at the agape love of God shed abroad in our hearts by the Holy Spirit. Define agape love and describe how it is different from the love we see in the world.

2. What is the most important truth you learned about agape love?

3. What was your favorite example of agape love in the reading today?

4. How does agape love make a difference in someone's life? How has agape love made a difference in your own life?

Day 15—He Reveals God's Word to You

1. What relationship does the Holy Spirit have to the Bible, the Word of God?

2. Why do we need the Holy Spirit when we read the Bible?

3. What are some practical ideas in day 15 that will help you read and study God's Word?

4. What did you learn from the example of Hannah Whitall Smith and her experience with the Bible?

5. What has been your own experience with the Bible? How has the Word of God made a difference in your life? How have you seen the Holy Spirit work in your own life with the Word of God?

Day 16—He Renews Your Heart

1. In day 16 you read about the renewing work of the Holy Spirit. What does it mean to be renewed within?

2. Why do we need spiritual renewal?

3. Have you ever experienced a spiritual renewal? If so, describe what it was like and how the Lord renewed you.

Day 17—He Sets Your Heart Free

1. In day 17 you looked at having a heart set free by the Holy Spirit. What does that mean?

2. Describe what freedom in Christ is and what it is not.

3. How has the Lord helped you to be more concerned with pleasing Him than with pleasing yourself?

4. What did you learn from the example of Richard Halverson? Why did he establish the Fellowship of the Burning Heart? What did it mean to be part of that fellowship?

Day 18—Quiet Time Week Three: Christ Lives in You

1. In day 18 you spent time thinking about the meaning of Christ living in you. What was the most significant verse you read today?

2. What does it mean to abide in Christ, and why are we to abide in Christ?

3. What was your favorite quote or insight from your quiet time?

4. What was the most important idea or truth you learned this week regarding the presence of the Holy Spirit in your life?

Week Four: The Power of the Holy Spirit
Day 19—Power for Personal Revival

1. We have been looking these last four weeks at who the Holy Spirit is and what He does. This week we looked at how the power of the Holy Spirit can make a difference in lives, both our own life and the lives of others. (As you lead your group through a discussion of each day in week 4, you may want to have someone read the verse at the beginning of each day.)

As you spent this week thinking about the power of the Holy

Spirit, what was the most important thing you learned? How did God speak to you this week?

2. What did you learn about personal spiritual revival? Why do we need to be revived?

3. Why is personal revival like a river of living water?

4. What will happen in your life when those rivers of living water begin to flow?

DAY 20—Power for Ministry

1. How does the Holy Spirit make a difference in ministry?

2. What is a spiritual gift, and why are we given spiritual gifts?

3. How are we to use our spiritual gifts?

4. What is the best way to discover your spiritual gift or gifts?

5. How has the Lord led you to use your own gifts in ministry?

DAY 21—Power for Difficult Circumstances

1. Why do we need the Holy Spirit in a difficulty or a trial? How does He make a difference in the impossible situations?

2. What did you learn about spiritual warfare, and how does the Holy Spirit make a difference when you are faced with a spiritual battle?

3. Has there been a time in your own life when the Holy Spirit has helped you in a difficulty or a trial?

4. What is your favorite phrase from "A Mighty Fortress Is Our God"?

DAY 22—Power for Prayer

1. Day 22 begins with this statement: "The Holy Spirit is your strength in prayer." How does the Holy Spirit help us in prayer?

2. What does "Abba Father" mean, and how does that phrase change the way you pray to your Lord?

3. How does the Holy Spirit help us even when we don't know what to pray?

Day 23—Power for Witnessing

1. How does the Holy Spirit make a difference when you tell others about Christ?

2. Why do we need the Holy Spirit when we witness for the Lord?

3. If you were going to tell someone else how to become a Christian, what would you share?

4. Briefly share in two or three minutes how you came to know Christ personally. (Have a few people in your group share their testimony briefly.)

5. Have you ever had a divine appointment and been given the opportunity to tell someone about the Lord? What happened, and how did you see the Lord at work?

Day 24—Quiet Time Week Four: I Can't, but He Can!

1. Why is the cry of the Christian "I can't, but He can"? What does that mean?

2. What was your favorite phrase in Ephesians 3:15-21?

3. What was the most important truth you learned from your quiet time? Was there a favorite quote from the John Henry Jowett excerpt?

4. Was there a favorite verse, quote, or insight from the entire week that you would like to share?

Week Five: The Purpose of the Holy Spirit
Day 25—He Makes You like Christ

1. What a journey it has been as we have explored the person of the Holy Spirit—who He is and what He does. You have

spent 30 days focusing on His power and your need for Him each and every day of your life. This is not really an ending but a beginning as you apply all you have learned about being filled with the Holy Spirit.

As you have now finished reading this book, what is the most important thing you've learned as a result of the journey? How will this book and its emphasis on the power of the Holy Spirit make a difference in your life? How has it changed the way you will live each day of your life?

2. In day 25 you had the opportunity to think about how the Holy Spirit transforms you from within and makes you like Christ. When He transforms you, what will happen in your life as a result?

3. What did you learn from the example of Chuck Colson?

4. How have you seen the Holy Spirit's transformation process at work in your own life in this last year?

Day 26—He Guides Your Steps

1. What did you learn about the Holy Spirit's leading and guidance in life?

2. How have you seen His guidance in your own life?

3. What meant the most to you about the example of J. Edwin Orr? How does his life and example challenge you?

Day 27—He Brings Unity to the Church

1. In day 27 you had the opportunity to look at what the Holy Spirit does in the church. How does He make a difference in the church?

2. What are ways the Holy Spirit works in the church?

3. What is His desire for the church?

4. We looked at the message the Holy Spirit had for the churches of western Asia minor in Revelation 2–3. What were the two main dangers described in Ephesus and Laodicea? How and why are those dangers facing the church today?

5. What will help us not to compromise or become complacent?

6. Did you have a chance to look at the spiritual goals worksheet? Were you able to write out some spiritual goals, and if so, could you share any with the group?

7. What difference can setting spiritual goals make in a person's life?

DAY 28—He Ignites Corporate Revivals

1. What happens when the Holy Spirit causes corporate revival? What does that look like?

2. What happened during the Isle of Lewis Revival in 1949?

3. Do you think that the Holy Spirit can cause this kind of revival again in the place where you live? Are you willing to pray and ask Him to revive the hearts of those in your home, neighborhood, church, and country?

DAY 29—Becoming an Instrument of Revival

1. In day 29 you looked at becoming a person God can use—an instrument of revival. How can you become a person the Lord can use?

2. As you think about all you've learned over these last 30 days, describe what it means to have a heart on fire. How can you have a heart on fire, and what difference can a heart on fire make in the world?

3. What will it mean to you to be part of the Fellowship of Hearts on Fire, to step out of the crowd and say, *Yes, Lord, I want to live for you and have a heart on fire for you?* (This is a personal question, but some people may like to share what this has meant to them.)

DAY 30—Quiet Time Week Five: Let the Rivers of Living Water Flow

1. How did the Lord use Evan Roberts in Wales in 1904–1905? Why do you think He was able to use Evan Roberts?

2. How is the Holy Spirit like a river of living water when He is at work in a life?

3. As you think about your journey over the last 30 days, what has been most significant to you?

4. What is the most important thing you have learned in this 30-day journey? What will you take with you from this time?

5. How was the letter you wrote to the Lord in day 1 answered during these last 30 days?

6. Who was your favorite example, what was your favorite verse, or favorite quote?

7. Is there anything else you would like to share as a result of your 30-day journey?

   Close in prayer.

THIRTY-ONE VERSES TO HELP YOU WALK IN THE SPIRIT

⋙

There are many verses on the Holy Spirit. Memorize these verses so they will always be available for you at any time. You might want to meditate on one each day for the next 31 days. You might even look at each verse in other translations, commentaries, and the *Treasury of Scripture Knowledge.* If you have the *Quiet Time Notebook,* you can use a Read and Study page or a Journal page for each verse.

> I will put My Spirit within you and cause you to walk in My statutes, and you will be careful to observe My ordinances (Ezekiel 36:27).

> "Not by might nor by power, but by My Spirit," says the LORD of hosts (Zechariah 4:6).

> Jesus answered, "Truly, truly, I say to you, unless one is born of water and the Spirit he cannot enter the kingdom of God" (John 3:5).

The wind blows where it wishes and you hear the sound of it, but do not know where it comes from and where it is going; so is everyone who is born of the Spirit (John 3:8).

For He whom God has sent speaks the words of God; for He gives the Spirit without measure (John 3:34).

It is the Spirit who gives life; the flesh profits nothing; the words that I have spoken to you are spirit and are life (John 6:63).

Now on the last day, the great day of the feast, Jesus stood and cried out, saying, "If anyone is thirsty, let him come to Me and drink. He who believes in Me, as the Scripture said, 'From his innermost being will flow rivers of living water.'" But this He spoke of the Spirit, whom those who believed in Him were to receive; for the Spirit was not yet given, because Jesus was not yet glorified (John 7:37-39).

I will ask the Father, and He will give you another Helper, that He may be with you forever; that is the Spirit of truth, whom the world cannot receive, because it does not see Him or know Him, but you know Him because He abides with you and will be in you (John 14:16-17).

But the Helper, the Holy Spirit, whom the Father will send in My name, He will teach you all things, and bring to your remembrance all that I said to you (John 14:26).

When the Helper comes, whom I will send to you from the Father, that is the Spirit of truth who proceeds from the Father, He will testify about Me (John 15:26).

But when He, the Spirit of truth, comes, He will guide you into all the truth; for He will not speak on His own initiative, but whatever He hears, He will speak; and He will disclose to you what is to come (John 16:13).

You will receive power when the Holy Spirit has come upon

you; and you shall be My witnesses both in Jerusalem, and in all Judea and Samaria, and even to the remotest part of the earth (Acts 1:8).

And the disciples were continually filled with joy and with the Holy Spirit (Acts 13:52).

Hope does not disappoint, because the love of God has been poured out within our hearts through the Holy Spirit who was given to us (Romans 5:5).

But now we have been released from the Law, having died to that by which we were bound, so that we serve in newness of the Spirit and not in the oldness of the letter (Romans 7:6).

However, you are not in the flesh but in the Spirit, if indeed the Spirit of God dwells in you. But if anyone does not have the Spirit of Christ, he does not belong to him (Romans 8:9).

For all who are being led by the Spirit of God, these are sons of God (Romans 8:14).

The Spirit Himself testifies with our spirit that we are children of God (Romans 8:16).

In the same way the Spirit also helps our weakness; for we do not know how to pray as we should, but the Spirit Himself intercedes for us with groanings too deep for words; and He who searches the hearts knows what the mind of the Spirit is, because He intercedes for the saints according to the will of God (Romans 8:26-27).

For the kingdom of God is not eating and drinking, but righteousness and peace and joy in the Holy Spirit (Romans 14:17).

Now may the God of hope fill you with all joy and peace in believing, so that you will abound in hope by the power of the Holy Spirit (Romans 15:13).

Now we have received, not the spirit of the world, but the Spirit who is from God, so that we may know the things freely given to us by God (1 Corinthians 2:12).

Do you not know that you are a temple of God and that the Spirit of God dwells in you? (1 Corinthians 3:16).

To each one is given the manifestation of the Spirit for the common good (1 Corinthians 12:7).

For by one Spirit we were all baptized into one body, whether Jews or Greeks, whether slaves or free, and we were all made to drink of one Spirit (1 Corinthians 12:13).

[God] also sealed us and gave us the Spirit in our hearts as a pledge (2 Corinthians 1:22).

Because you are sons, God has sent forth the Spirit of His Son into our hearts, crying "Abba! Father!" (Galatians 4:6).

But the fruit of the Spirit is love, joy, peace, patience, kindness, goodness, faithfulness, gentleness, self-control; against such things there is no law. Now those who belong to Christ Jesus have crucified the flesh with its passions and desires. If we live by the Spirit, let us also walk by the Spirit (Galatians 5:22-25).

And do not get drunk with wine, for that is dissipation, but be filled with the Spirit (Ephesians 5:18).

By this we know that we abide in Him and He in us, because He has given us of His Spirit (1 John 4:13).

The Spirit and the bride say, "Come." And let the one who hears say, "Come." And let the one who is thirsty come; let the one who wishes take the water of life without cost (Revelation 22:17).

Appendix 3

SPIRITUAL GIFTS

≫

M any books are available on the Holy Spirit and specifically on the gifts of the Holy Spirit. Scholars and authors differ on the number of gifts and their descriptions. Charles Ryrie lists 14 spiritual gifts, Leslie Flynn lists 19, and Peter Wagner lists 27. With that in mind, the following description of spiritual gifts is not meant to be exhaustive but instructive and helpful in understanding of the gifts of the Spirit.

Three main passages of Scripture refer to gifts of the Spirit: Romans 12:3-8; 1 Corinthians 12:27-28; and Ephesians 4:7-16. Two main Greek words are used for spiritual gifts. First, *pneumatikos* is used in 1 Corinthians 12:1 and refers to those graces and things given to man from the Holy Spirit. These gifts are not natural talents but spiritual and come from the Spirit. Second, *charisma* is used in Romans 12:6 and denotes a divine enablement imparted by God through the Holy Spirit in the life of the believer for the edification of others. William McRae defines a spiritual gift as "a divine endowment of a special ability for service upon a member of the body of Christ."[1]

All Christians are members of the church, the body of Christ. As such, each believer is designed by God for a particular function and place of service within the body of Christ. The gifts of the Spirit are divine enablements to serve in the ways God has planned and designed for each believer. Paul used the analogy of the human body: "For just as we have many members in one body and all the members do not have the same function, so we, who are many, are one body in Christ, and individually members one of another. Since we have gifts that differ according to the grace given to us, each of us is to exercise them accordingly" (Romans 12:4-6). Paul makes some very important statements in 1 Corinthians 12 about the function of the body of Christ and the exercise of gifts:

> For the body is not one member, but many…But now God has placed the members, each one of them, in the body, just as He desired…If they were all one member, where would the body be? But now there are many members, but one body…so that there may be no division in the body, but that the members may have the same care for one another… Now you are Christ's body, and individually members of it.

These verses clarify the fact that you cannot think about spiritual gifts apart from the context of the church, the body of Christ. God gives you gifts so you can serve Him in the church. Understand that you have a high calling and purpose from God within the church, also called the bride of Christ. No position is any higher than another position—each one is necessary and important in God's economy. Therefore, all believers should serve the Lord with all their heart in the ways God leads as they are filled with the Holy Spirit. You can count on God to be faithful to lead you to those ministries where He desires for you to serve. Launch out on His promises, rely on His power, and rejoice in His work in and through you.

The Bible mentions these gifts:

Wisdom (Greek, *sophia* in 1 Corinthians 12:8). This wisdom is the supernatural ability given by the Holy Spirit to apply knowledge from the mind of Christ discovered in the Word of God to specific needs in the body of Christ.[2]

Knowledge (Greek, *gnosis* in 1 Corinthians 12:8). The gift of knowledge is a supernatural ability given by the Holy Spirit to know, understand, and explain God's revelation in the Scriptures and in creation.[3]

Faith (Greek, *pistis* in 1 Corinthians 12:9). Faith is the supernatural ability to trust God to carry out what He says in His Word. This faith is not a reference to saving faith (Ephesians 2:8) as all Christians exercise this kind of faith. The spiritual gift of faith is the kind of faith Jesus describes as able to move mountains (Matthew 17:20).

Healing (Greek, *iama* in 1 Corinthians 12:9). Healing is a supernatural work of God on behalf of those experiencing affliction and disease. We see the application of the work of God in healing in James 5:14-16, where the elders of the church are instructed to pray for those who are sick.

> When these people [elders] claim the words written by James and trust that God will hear and answer their earnest prayer, the miracle of healing frequently occurs. We make two cautionary remarks, however: first, these elders should not expect that they have received a permanent gift to heal every member of the church who is ill; next, in spite of fervent prayer offered in faith, God may choose not to restore someone to normal health and strength.[4]

Miracles (Greek, *energema dunamis* in 1 Corinthians 12:10). The supernatural work of God to perform an act contrary to the laws of nature. In the exercise of a miracle, God is the agent and the instrument is man.

Prophecy (Greek, *propheteia* in 1 Corinthians 12:10,28). Prophecy is the supernatural ability given by the Holy Spirit to proclaim the plans and purposes of God as seen in the Word of God. Prophecy confirms what God says in His Word and never adds to Scripture.

Discerning of spirits (Greek, *diakrisis pneuma* in 1 Corinthians 12:10). The supernatural ability given by the Holy Spirit to discern whether something is truth from God in His Word or false teaching.

Tongues (Greek, *glossa* in 1 Corinthians 12:10,28). The supernatural ability given by the Holy Spirit to speak in a language or utterance unknown to the speaker. On the day of Pentecost the disciples spoke in languages they didn't know but that those from other parts of the world clearly understood (see Acts 2). Commentator Alan Johnson relates this story about the Rev. Ruolneikhum (Kuhma) Pakhuongte, president of the Free Churches of India.

> Once he was asked to preach the gospel to a small, unevangelized village in the Assam province of eastern India. When he arrived, he discovered that the local residents spoke only in a language that he did not know. There was no interpreter. Rather than return home, he was led by the Holy Spirit to preach to them for two hours in his own language. At the close of his message, he asked them to turn to Christ for salvation. To his amazement, the entire village responded to his invitation to receive Jesus as their Lord. Later he learned that they had all heard him speak in their own language during those two hours. Kuhma said this has never happened in his ministry before or since.[5]

Interpretation of tongues (Greek, *hermeneia glossa* in 1 Corinthians 12:10; 14:13). The supernatural ability given by the Holy Spirit to understand and explain what the speaker has said in a language unknown to the speaker or the listener.

Apostle (Greek, *apostolos* in Ephesians 4:11). Some systematic theologians differentiate between the *gift* and the *office* of the apostle.[6] The office of apostle with its unique authority granted by Jesus is limited to those who were eyewitnesses of Jesus, such as Paul and the 12 disciples. Bill Bright defines the one with the gift of apostle as "one who is gifted by the Holy Spirit with the special ability to give leadership to a number of churches and to show supernatural wisdom and authority in spiritual matters that relate to those churches."[7]

Teaching (Greek, *didaskalia* in Romans 12:7; 1 Corinthians 12:28; Ephesians 4:11). The supernatural ability given by the Holy Spirit to teach truth from the Word of God in such a way that it is easily understandable and applicable in the lives of those who are taught.

Helps (Greek, *antilepsis* in 1 Corinthians 12:28). This supernatural gift given by the Holy Spirit is the ability to lend assistance and is usually task oriented.

Service (Greek, *diakonia* in Romans 12:7). This supernatural gift given by the Holy Spirit is the ability to give care to practical needs of those in the church and is usually people oriented. The English term *deacon* comes from this Greek word.

Mercy (Greek, *eleeo* in Romans 12:8). This supernatural gift given by the Holy Spirit is the ability to aid the infirm, afflicted, hungry, or elderly.

Administration (Greek, *kybernesis* in 1 Corinthians 12:28). The Greek word used here refers to a pilot or helmsman. This gift given by the Holy Spirit enables one to hold the helm of a church, formulate strategies, and also steer the church through troubled or choppy waters.

Leadership (Greek, *proistemi* in Romans 12:8). The Greek word means "government" and is the ability given by the Holy Spirit to manage in the church and take care of the church. One who has the gift of leadership is able to set goals and motivate and direct others to work toward accomplishing those goals.

Exhortation (Greek, *paraklesis* in Romans 12:8). This supernatural gift given by the Holy Spirit is the ability to come alongside others and help them by building them up, comforting, and consoling them.

Giving (Greek, *metadidomi* in Romans 12:8). The supernatural ability given by the Holy Spirit to make money and contribute financially to carry out the work of God in the church.

Evangelist (Greek, *euaggelistes* in Ephesians 4:11). Some people in the church are evangelists, and they are enabled by the Spirit of God to proclaim the good news of the gospel. All believers in church are armed with the Great Commission in Matthew 28:18-20 to tell others about Christ (2 Timothy 4:5). Those who are evangelists possess a supernatural ability to "proclaim the Good News of salvation effectively so that people respond to the claims of Christ in conversion and in discipleship."[8]

Pastor (Greek, *poimen* in Ephesians 4:11). The supernatural ability given by the Holy Spirit to shepherd others in the church.

Ray Stedman shares the following perspective about how we serve the Lord:

> I am a son of God among the sons of men. I am equipped with the power of God to labor today. In the very work given me today God will be with me, doing it through me. I am gifted with special abilities to help people in various areas, and I don't have to wait until Sunday to use these gifts. I can use them anywhere. I can exercise the gift God has given me as soon as I find out what it is, by taking note of my desires and by asking others what they see in me and by trying out various things. I am going to set myself to the lifelong task of keeping that gift busy.[9]

Paul told Timothy, "Kindle afresh the gift of God which is in you" (2 Timothy 1:6). William McRae, in his book on spiritual gifts, shares the same attitude:

> That is exactly what you should do. You have a gift. The rest of the body needs it. You will be accountable for what you do with it. Use it so that one day you will hear Jesus say, "Well done, good and faithful servant! You have been faithful with a few things; I will put you in charge of many things. Come and share your master's happiness" (Matthew 25:21,23).[10]

SPIRITUAL GOALS

Draw near to the Lord and ask Him to guide you as you write out your spiritual goals for the year. You might want to read a few passages of Scripture as you prepare for this time of planning: Psalm 1; 25; 27; 84.

Goals for My Relationship with God

What would I like to see happen in my relationship with the Lord?

What qualities of Christ (fruit of the Spirit) will I focus on?

When and where will I spend quiet time with the Lord?

What is my Bible reading plan for this year?

Which devotional books will I include in my quiet time?

What other tools will I use in my quiet time? (Check out *Six Secrets to a Powerful Quiet Time* and *Knowing and Loving the Bible* to help you in this.)

How will I study the Bible this year? (What book of the Bible or topic would you like to focus on this year? What Bible study book or tools will you use to help you?)

What books will I read this year?

How will I grow in my prayer life this year?

How will I memorize more Scripture this year?

What important verses will I focus on this year?

What important words will I focus on this year?

Goals for My Relationships with Others
How I can encourage my family in the Lord this year?

How will I grow in my friendships and fellowship this year?

Goals for My Ministry in the Church
How I can use my gifts this year?

How I can serve in my church this year?

What are some new ideas for ministry?

Which ministry ideas will I work on this year?

How will I grow in the area of sharing my faith with others? (Maybe you'd like to write out your testimony or learn the Four Spiritual Laws.)

Appendix 5

THE FELLOWSHIP OF HEARTS ON FIRE

≫

Dear friend, let's join together in this fellowship of hearts on fire as those who desire to be sold out for Christ, wholeheartedly committed to Him, and living for Him as long as we have breath. Making these commitments is a decisive resolve to give ourselves to God, knowing that "the eyes of the Lord move to and fro throughout the earth that He may strongly support those whose heart is completely His" (2 Chronicles 16:9). May our God "count you worthy of your calling, and fulfill every desire for goodness and work of faith with power, so that the name of our Lord Jesus will be glorified in you, and you in Him, according to the grace of our God and the Lord Jesus Christ" (2 Thessalonians 1:11-12).

Commitment 1: Lord, I commit myself to radical intimacy.

I AM COMMITTED TO THE PROMISE FROM YOU that when I draw near to You, You will draw near to me (James 4:8). I desire and resolve to spend daily quiet time alone with You, reading and studying Your Word, talking with You in prayer, and meditating on devotional reading.

Commitment 2: Lord, I commit myself to radical authority.

I AM COMMITTED TO THE PROMISE FROM YOU that all Scripture is inspired by You and profitable for teaching, for reproof, for correction, and for training in righteousness, so that I may be adequate and equipped for every good work (2 Timothy 3:16-17). I desire and resolve to turn to You in Your Word to discover what is true and desire and resolve to live by what You say in the Bible rather than being controlled by the world, my feelings, or other circumstances.

Commitment 3: Lord, I commit myself to radical revival.

I AM COMMITTED TO THE PROMISE FROM YOU that I, with unveiled face, beholding as in a mirror Your glory, am being transformed into the same image from glory to glory, just as from the Lord, the Spirit (2 Corinthians 3:18) and that when I come to You, Lord Jesus, and believe in You, You will cause rivers of living water to flow from my innermost being (John 7:37-38). I desire and resolve to be revived personally and spiritually day by day and to live like You, Lord Jesus, instead of living like the world.

Commitment 4: Lord, I commit myself to radical power.

I AM COMMITTED TO THE PROMISE FROM YOU that I will receive power when the Holy Spirit has come upon me and that You desire me to be Your witness in Jerusalem, and in all Judea and Samaria, and even to the remotest part of the earth (Acts 1:8). I desire and resolve to live in the power of the Holy Spirit and will tell others the good news about You through my life and witness.

Commitment 5: Lord, I commit myself to radical discipleship.

I AM COMMITTED TO THE PROMISE FROM YOU that by Your mercies, You desire me to present my body a living and holy sacrifice, acceptable to You, which is my spiritual service of worship (Romans 12:1). I desire and resolve to surrender all of myself to You as a living sacrifice, recklessly abandoned to Your will and living for You.

I desire to make these commitments before You, Lord, and rely on the Holy Spirit to help me run the race You have set before me. *Lord, set my heart on fire.*

Name _____

Date _____

NOTES

INTRODUCTION

1. A.W. Tozer, *The Knowledge of the Holy* (New York: Harper & Row, 1961), p. 6.

DAY 1

1. From Moody's comments at Spurgeon's Jubilee Testimonial Service in London on June 18, 1886. Available online at members.aol.com/pilgrimpub/hayden.htm.

DAY 2

1. Charles Spurgeon, *Morning and Evening* (Scotland: Christian Focus Publications, 1994), November 4 a.m.

DAY 3

1. Simon J. Kistemaker and William Hendriksen, *New Testament Commentary,* vol. 17, *Exposition of the Acts of the Apostles* (Grand Rapids: Baker Book House, 2001), p. 77.

2. Lewis Sperry Chafer, *He That Is Spiritual* (Grand Rapids: Zondervan, 1918), pp. 26-27.

3. Cleon L. Rogers Jr. and Cleon L. Rogers III, *The New Linguistic and Exegetical Key to the Greek New Testament* (Grand Rapids: Zondervan, 1998), p. 584.

4. Chafer, *He That Is Spiritual,* pp. 43-44.

5. Bill Bright, "How to Be Filled with the Holy Spirit" in *Here's Life Open Bible* (San Bernardino, CA: Campus Crusade for Christ, 1979), p. 11.

6. Quoted in Leona Choy, *The Life-Changing Power of the Holy Spirit* (Camp Hill, PA: Christian Publications, 2003), p. 237.

7. Ibid., pp. 199-200.

8. John Henry Jowett, *The Eagle Life* (New York: George H. Doran, 1922), pp. 12-14.

9. Ibid., p. 106.

10. A.J. Appasamy, *Write the Vision* (Fort Washington, PA: Christian Literature Crusade, 1964), p. 219.

DAY 4

1. A.B. Simpson, *The Holy Spirit* (Camp Hill, PA: Christian Publications, n.d.) p. 132.

2. Mrs. Charles Cowman, *Streams in the Desert* (Los Angeles: The Oriental Missionary Society, 1955), pp. 168-69.

DAY 5

1. James McConkey, *The Three-fold Secret of the Holy Spirit* (Pittsburgh: Silver Publishing Society, 1897), p. 86.

2. Annie Johnson Flint, "The Set of the Sail," in *Best-Loved Poems* (Toronto: Evangelical Press), pp. 18-19.

DAY 6

1. F.B. Meyer, *The Bells of Is* (London: Marshall, Morgan & Scott Ltd., 1928), p. 17.

2. See Warren W. Wiersbe, *Living with the Giants* (Grand Rapids: Baker Book House, 1993), p. 146.

3. F.B. Meyer, *Great Verses Through The Bible* (Grand Rapids: Zondervan, 1972), pp. 417-18.

DAY 7

1. See Catherine Martin, *Knowing and Loving the Bible* (Eugene, OR: Harvest House, 2007), p. 80.

2. J. Oswald Sanders, *The Holy Spirit of Promise* (London: Marshall, Morgan & Scott, 1954), p. 33.

DAY 8

1. Quoted in F. Raymond Edman, *They Found the Secret* (Grand Rapids: Zondervan, 1984), pp. 41-44.

DAY 9

1. Leon Morris, *The New International Commentary on the New Testament,* vol. 4, *The Gospel According to John* (Grand Rapids: Eerdmans, 1971), p. 662.

2. F.B. Meyer, *Gospel of John* (Fort Washington, PA: Christian Literature Crusade, 1992), p. 235.

3. Charles Spurgeon, *Morning and Evening* (Scotland: Christian Focus Publications, 1994), January 16 a.m.

DAY 10

1. Dr. and Mrs. Howard Taylor, *Hudson Taylor's Spiritual Secret* (New Kensington, PA: Whitaker House, 1996), p. 15.

DAY 11

1. David Martyn Lloyd-Jones, *God's Ultimate Purpose* (Carlisle, PA: Banner of Truth, 1978), p. 309.

DAY 12

1. Warren W. Wiersbe, *Living with the Giants* (Grand Rapids: Baker Book House, 1993), p. 224.

2. A.W. Tozer, *The Christian Book of Mystical Verse* (Camp Hill, PA: Christian Publications, 1963), p. vi.

3. Quoted in Warren Wiersbe, *The Best of A. W. Tozer,* vol. 2 (Camp Hill, PA: Christian Publications, n.d.), p. 40.

4. F.B. Meyer, *Daily Prayers* (Wheaton, IL: Harold Shaw, 1995), p. 7.

5. Quoted in Wiersbe, *The Best of A.W. Tozer,* pp. 47-48.

DAY 13

1. Bruce Marchiano, *In the Footsteps of Jesus* (Eugene, OR: Harvest House, 1997), p. 133.

2. Andrew A. Bonar and R.M. McCheyne, *Memoir and Remains of R.M. McCheyne* (Chicago: Moody Press, 1996), p. 294.

DAY 14

1. From James S. Hewett, *Illustrations Unlimited* (Wheaton: Tyndale House, 1988), p. 74.

2. Andrew Murray, *The Secret of Spiritual Strength* (New Kensington, PA: Whitaker House, 1997), p. 36.

3. Charles Spurgeon, *Morning and Evening* (Scotland: Christian Focus Publications, 1994), June 11 a.m.

DAY 15

1. Fritz Rienecker and Cleon L. Rogers, *Linguistic Key to the Greek New Testament* (Grand Rapids: Zondervan, 1982).

2. Paul Enns, *Moody Handbook of Theology* (Chicago: Moody Press, 1989), p. 175.

3. The best selection of sermons I have found is available online at www.sermonindex.net. I especially recommend that you listen to all of J. Edwin Orr's sermons there and at www.jedwinorr.com.

4. Hannah Whitall Smith, *The Unselfishness of God* (New York: Fleming H. Revell, 1903), pp. 190-91.

5. Ibid., pp. 191-93.

DAY 16

1. David E. Garland, *The New American Commentary,* vol. 29, *2 Corinthians* (Nashville: Broadman & Holman Publishers, 2001), p. 241.

2. George B. Caird, quoted in Garland, *2 Corinthians,* p. 241.

3. Annie Johnson Flint, "My Wings," in *Best-Loved Poems by Annie Johnson Flint* (Toronto: Evangelical Press, n.d.), pp. 129-30.

DAY 18

1. Amy Carmichael, *Mountain Breezes* (Fort Washington, PA: Christian Literature Crusade, 1999), p. 182.

2. Andrew Murray, *The True Vine* (Springdale, PA: Whitaker House, 1982), pp. 31-32.

DAY 19

1. Geoffrey W. Bromiley, *The International Standard Bible Encyclopedia,* revised ed., vol. 1 (Grand Rapids: Eerdmans, 2002), p. 725.

2. Brian H. Edwards, *Revival* (Durham, England: Evangelical Press, 1990), p. 65.

3. Matthew Henry, *Matthew Henry's Commentary on the Whole Bible* (Peabody: Hendrickson, 1996), q.v. 2 Kings 22:11.

DAY 20

1. Charles Spurgeon, *Morning and Evening* (Scotland: Christian Focus Publications, 1994), October 21 a.m.

2. Ray Stedman, *The Body at Work* (Palo Alto, CA: Discovery Publishing, a ministry of Peninsula Bible Church, 1995), p. 7.

DAY 21

1. David Martyn Lloyd-Jones, *The Christian Soldier* (Carlisle, PA: Banner of Truth, 1977), p. 22.

2. William Gurnall, *The Christian in Complete Armour* (Carlisle, PA: The Banner of Truth Trust, 1989), p. 34.

DAY 22

1. Fritz Rienecker and Cleon L. Rogers, *Linguistic Key to the Greek New Testament* (Grand Rapids: Zondervan, 1982), p. 367.

DAY 24

1. F.B. Meyer, *Daily Prayers* (Wheaton, IL: Harold Shaw, 1995), p. 103.

2. John Henry Jowett, *The Silver Lining* (New York: Fleming H. Revell, 1907), pp. 192-94.

DAY 27

1. R.C. Sproul, *The Soul's Quest for God* (Wheaton, IL: Tyndale House, 1996), p. 200.

2. J.I. Packer, *Growing in Christ* (Wheaton, IL: Crossway Books, 1996), p. 17.

3. Marshall Shelley, ed., *Growing Your Church Through Training and Motivation* (Minneapolis: Bethany House, 1997), p. 45.

4. Bill Bright, *How You Can Help Fulfill the Great Commission*, audio transcript (San Bernardino, CA: Campus Crusade for Christ International, 1990).

5. Quoted in Leona Choy, *The Life-Changing Power of the Holy Spirit* (Camp Hill, PA: Christian Publications, 2003), p. 312.

DAY 29

1. Quoted in Leona Choy, *The Life-Changing Power of the Holy Spirit* (Camp Hill, PA: Christian Publications, 2003), p. 217.

2. Brian Edwards, *Revival* (Darlington, England: Evangelical Press, 1994), p. 46.

DAY 30

1. Mrs. Charles Cowman, *Springs in the Valley* (Los Angeles: The Oriental Missionary Society, 1939), p. 175.

APPENDIX 3: SPIRITUAL GIFTS

1. William McRae, *The Dynamics of Spiritual Gifts* (Grand Rapids: Zondervan, 1976), p. 18.

2. See Bill Bright, *The Holy Spirit* (Orlando: NewLife Publications, 1980), p. 257.

3. See Simon J. Kistemaker and William Hendriksen, *New Testament Commentary*, vol. 18, *Exposition of the First Epistle to the Corinthians* (Grand Rapids: Baker Book House, 2001), p. 421.

4. Ibid.

5. Alan F. Johnson, *The IVP New Testament Commentary Series*, vol. 7, *1 Corinthians* (Downers Grove, IL.: InterVarsity Press, 2004), p. 227.

6. Paul Enns, *The Moody Handbook of Theology* (Chicago: Moody Press, 1989), p. 270.

7. Bill Bright, *The Holy Spirit* (Orlando: NewLife, 1980), p. 261.

8. Leslie B. Flynn, *19 Gifts of the Spirit* (Wheaton, IL: Victor Books, 1974), p. 57.

9. Ray Stedman, "Who Am I, Lord?" Sermon delivered on March 13, 1977, p. 7.

10. William McRae, *The Dynamics of Spiritual Gifts* (Grand Rapids: Zondervan, 1976), p. 18.

ACKNOWLEDGMENTS

First, I thank the Lord, who gave me the idea for this book and its title and who led and guided me as I wrote. I thank Him for the incredible gift of the Comforter, the Holy Spirit, who gives me the ability to say, "I can't, but He can!"

The Lord has blessed me with the most incredible family a girl could ever have. Thank you, David, my dear husband, for helping me in so many ways with this book. I thank the Lord for your discernment and skill in editing and for your brilliance every step of the way. It was so much fun journeying through this book with you.

I am so thankful to my mother, Elizabeth Snyder, and my dad, Robert Snyder, for your love and encouragement of me in the good times and the difficult times. Rob and Tania, thank you for your love and support. Christopher, I'm so proud of you, and dear Kayla, you are the apple of my eye, and I am praying for you to live for the Lord in your generation for such a time as this. Eloise, thank you for loving and encouraging me.

The Lord has given me the privilege of having many friends and colaborers who have hearts on fire for Him. Thank you to my dear friends who love me, challenge me, encourage me and teach me: Andy Graybill, Beverly Trupp, Cindy Clark, Conni Hudson, Shirley Peters, Kelly Abeyratne, Julie Airis, Helen Peck, Stefanie Kelly, Carolyn Haynes, Myra Murphy, John and Betty Mann, Paula Zillmer, Kayla Branscum, Vonette Bright, and Josh and Dottie McDowell.

A special thank you to my assistant at Quiet Time Ministries, Kayla Branscum, who works tirelessly above and beyond in serving the Lord. Kayla, thank you for using your gifts to serve the Lord, to help me in a thousand ways, and for connecting with people literally all over the world about quiet time. Thank you to the Quiet Time Ministries team who meets weekly to pray for me and all aspects of Quiet Time Ministries. Thank you to those volunteers, especially Paula Zillmer, who have helped us publish quiet time resources, send out mailings, and fulfill so many other aspects of this ministry.

Thank you to the board of directors of Quiet Time Ministries—David Martin, Conni Hudson, Shirley Peters, and Jane Lyons—for engaging in this journey with me as the Lord continues to open amazing doors of ministry to teach devotion to God and His Word to men and women throughout the world. Thank you to the *Enriching Your Quiet Time* magazine team of writers and editors—Shirley Peters, Conni Hudson, Cay Hough, and Maurine Cromwell—who have been helpful in developing ideas for my books through articles and quiet times. A special thank you to those who partner financially and prayerfully with Quiet Time Ministries.

Thank you to Shelley Smith, our Women's Ministries assistant at Southwest Community Church, for helping me and serving our women so faithfully. Thank you to the women at Southwest for your faithfulness to the Lord. It is a joy to serve with you. Thank you to Pastor Bob Thune and to our adult ministries staff team: Pastor Mark Wold, Pastor Jim Smoke, Pastor Pablo Cachon, Abner Lima, Shelley Smith, and Caroline Sharpe.

Thank you to those who piloted *Set My Heart on Fire:* Conni Hudson, for leading the pilot in Bermuda Dunes, California, and to Shirley Baker, Kayla Branscum, Melissa Brown, Nancy Brown, Ceil Burns, Sheila Chadwick, Cheryle Clark, Cindy Clark, Donna Delahanty, Ada Elsner, Jenny Elsner, Loretta Harrell, Joan Hill, Sandra Hill, Leah Hudson, Dawn Ivie, Barbara Knopes, Davida Kreisler, Kristin Largent, Sally Leachman, Kay McCann, Shirley Peters, Kate Storset, Sherylen Yoak, Paula Zillmer, Julie Airis, Cay Hough, Betty Mann, Myra Murphy, Kathleen Otremba, Beverly Trupp, and Sharon Hastings. Your feedback, comments, and corrections were invaluable for the final version of *Set My Heart on Fire.*

Thank you to Jim Smoke, author and pastor, for being one of my great examples in life. You have taught me so much, and I thank the Lord for you. Thank you to Greg Johnson, of WordServe Literary Group, for encouraging me in Quiet Time Ministries and for representing me as my agent. Thank you to all the pastors, directors of women's ministries, and leaders who are faithfully teaching the Word of God. Your faithfulness is such an encouragement to me.

I am especially thankful for my wonderful publisher, Harvest House Publishers, who makes writing books one of the greatest joys in serving the Lord. Oh, how I thank the Lord for you. Thank you, Bob Hawkins Jr., for leading such an incredible team of men and women at Harvest House and for encouraging me to write the books that the Lord has placed on my heart.

Thank you to Terry Glaspey for your creativity and encouragement, Gene Skinner, for your impeccable editing of my books, Carolyn McCready, for your enthusiasm, Barb Sherrill, and Katie Lane for your vision for my books, Jeana Newman for making radio so much fun, Shane White, who makes it exciting to answer the phone, and so many others who are such a joy to serve with including LaRae Weikert, Steve Miller, John Constance, Betty Fletcher, Kimberly Shumate, and Peggy Wright. And finally, I want to thank Bob and Shirley Hawkins for faithfully serving the Lord all these years, working tirelessly in the publishing industry. Bob, the day I met you changed my life forever, and I will be eternally grateful. I'm so glad I was willing to set aside my own small idea and set my sail to catch the wind of the Holy Spirit as He opened the doors to get my books into the hands of thousands throughout the world. To God be the glory.

ABOUT THE AUTHOR

Catherine Martin is a summa cum laude graduate of Bethel Theological Seminary with a master of arts degree in theological studies. She is founder and president of Quiet Time Ministries, director of women's ministries at Southwest Community Church in Indian Wells, California, and adjunct faculty member of Biola University. She is the author of *Six Secrets to a Powerful Quiet Time, Knowing and Loving the Bible,* and *Walking with the God Who Cares,* published by Harvest House Publishers, and *Pilgrimage of the Heart, Revive My Heart!,* and *A Heart That Dances* published by NavPress. She has also written *The Quiet Time Notebook, A Heart on Fire, A Heart to See Forever, A Heart That Hopes in God,* and *Run Before the Wind,* published by Quiet Time Ministries Press. She is senior editor for *Enriching Your Quiet Time* quarterly magazine. As a popular speaker at retreats and conferences, Catherine challenges others to seek God and love Him with all of their heart, soul, mind, and strength. For more information about Catherine, visit www.quiettime.org, www.catherinemartinonline.com, and www.cathsblog.com.

About Quiet Time Ministries

Quiet Time Ministries is a nonprofit organization offering resources for your quiet time. Visit us online at www.quiettime.org. The Quiet Time Ministries Resource and Training Center, located in Bermuda Dunes, California, offers conferences and workshops to encourage others in their relationship with the Lord.

Quiet Time Ministries
Post Office Box 14007
Palm Desert, CA 92255
1-800-925-6458
760-772-2357
www.quiettime.org

OTHER *SET MY HEART ON FIRE* RESOURCES
available from Quiet Time Ministries

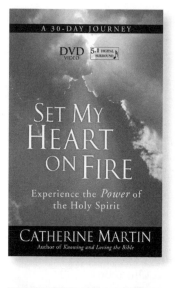

Companion DVD

This Companion DVD with six messages by Catherine Martin is designed to accompany your 30-day journey of *Set My Heart on Fire*. Each message is filled with inspiration and encouragement and is ideal for individuals or groups. The Companion DVD is available from Quiet Time Ministries online at www.quiettime.org or by phone at 1-800-925-6458.

Companion Journal

This Companion Journal is designed for use with your 30-day journey of *Set My Heart on Fire*. It contains journal and prayer pages taken from the *Quiet Time Notebook* published by Quiet Time Ministries Press. Also included are promise pages to "write a check" on the promise as described in *Set My Heart on Fire*. These pages will help you learn how to find the promise, embrace the promise, trust the promise, and live the promise. The Companion Journal is available from Quiet Time Ministries online at www.quiettime.org or by phone at 1-800-925-6458.